CRAFTFULNESS

CRAFT-FULNESS

Mend Yourself by

Making Things

Rosemary Davidson and Arzu Tahsin

HARPER WAVE

An Imprint of HarperCollinsPublishers

HarperCollins books may be purchased for educational, business, or sales promotional use. For information, please email the Special Markets Department at SPsales@harpercollins.com.

Originally published in Great Britain in 2018 by Quercus Editions Ltd.

FIRST U.S. EDITION

Illustrations by Amber Anderson

Title page illustrations by Bodor Tivadar/Shutterstock, Inc.

Library of Congress Cataloging-in-Publication Data

Names: Davidson, Rosemary, author. | Tahsin, Arzu, author.
Title: Craftfulness : mend yourself by making things / Rosemary Davidson and Arzu Tahsin.
Description: First edition. | New York : Harper Wave, [2019] | "Originally published as Craftfulness in Great Britain in 2018 by Quercus Editions Ltd."
Identifiers: LCCN 2018034447 | ISBN 9780062883544 (hardback)
Subjects: LCSH: Handicraft--Psychological aspects. | Self-actualization (Psychology) | BISAC: SELF-HELP / Personal Growth / Happiness. | SELF-HELP / Motivational & Inspirational. | CRAFTS & HOBBIES / General.
Classification: LCC TT14 .D38 2019 | DDC 745.5--dc23
LC record available at https://lccn.loc.gov/2018034447

19 20 21 22 23   LSC   10 9 8 7 6 5 4 3 2 1

For Esme & Will

CONTENTS

INTRODUCTION

The Tao of Making
(Or how we realised craft was our therapy)

'Working with my hands to make a thing – whether it's
a sketchbook or a piece of weaving or a drawing – fulfils
some essential function of me. It feels predestined, it's part
of my DNA. I can't imagine not having a project on the
go. There would be a hole in my life, a sense that there
is something I should be doing. When I'm making I am
focused, resolved, connected to the work I am shaping.
Afterwards, I feel refreshed, invigorated even, and always
more energetic for what is going on around me. I've come
to the conclusion that as long as I'm making, I can do all
the other things being alive requires of me. I equate my
daily craft practice with, if anything, meditation.'
– Arzu Tahsin, editor, crafter

'My granny was a seamstress in a department store
in Glasgow in the 1920s. Her brother was a machine
engineer at the Coats thread factory in Paisley and she
had these old boxes at the bottom of her wardrobe full
of spools of cotton in a whole palette of gorgeous colours.

There were beads, bits of jet, feathers and fantastic treasures she'd hoarded for years. I loved her stories of the smart city ladies she sewed for and dreamed of fairy-tale outfits I'd make with the motley coloured threads; that's what gave me the itch to make. When I'm making I have room to think. And to do my daydreaming.'
— *Rosemary Davidson, editor, crafter*

It was late November, too early for the Christmas spirit to have really kicked in, but close enough to panic that the scarves we were knitting wouldn't be finished in time to give as presents. So, as well as dinner and gossip, we added knitting to that evening's agenda.

As we finished one row and cast on another, our conversation meandered around family and work and their respective joys and frustrations, and from there to general musings on the pleasure of just sitting around making stuff, and losing yourself in an activity that doesn't require too much thought. We talked not just about knitting, but anything that you can do with your hands that feels almost automatic. We remarked on our compulsion to *make things* and where this desire came from. We compared how we each felt during the process and agreed that the activity itself provided additional, but elusive benefits, beyond the satisfaction of having created a physical object.

We realised that the two of us have been crafters for almost as long as we've had hands. Through marriage, divorce, various jobs, mental health issues and the ups and downs of raising young children, we have consistently crafted. We have used our creativity to bring to life the ideas in our heads, whether it's by knitting, crochet, bookbinding, weaving, potting plants or making ceramics; sitting in Rosemary's kitchen, we acknowledged to each other that it has become as essential to us as putting on clothes in order to leave the house.

We're both avid readers, and we chatted about how there are many books about craftsmanship, on the joy and positive effects of working with your hands for a living. Between us, we had read several memoirs by skilled craftsmen and women who have spent a lifetime honing their expertise to perfection in order to produce exquisite furniture or pottery. But we realised that we also wanted to read about ordinary, everyday craft, the simple pleasure to be had just from making stuff, without worrying too much about how it turns out, and how it makes us feel. A book that included the stories and experiences of people like us who work in quite different areas to the crafts they pursue, yet pursue them all the same.

Why do we craft? What is to be gained from spending regular periods of time absorbed in a creative pastime? Given that neither one of us is necessarily interested in setting up a business and selling pinch pots and rag dolls, what is the point?

Before long we had some answers to these questions that had evolved over that November evening, and began to put together some thoughts. We make things because we enjoy it *and* because our crafts make us feel better. It is when we return to our sewing, knitting, bookbinding or weaving that we achieve moments of calm. When our energy is low, making something energises us. When we feel overwhelmed or stressed, crafting returns us to an even keel – it helps to keep the different demands on our time in balance. Making reaches into the place where ideas are sparked and where problems are resolved. Our crafts add meaning and purpose, along with new challenges and the drive to gain skills and mastery, in our lives. And because making something from scratch often leads us to new experiences, new encounters and new areas of imaginative inquiry, interest and inspiration, we feel more engaged and generally more effective in our work and relationships as a result. As long as we are making and creatively fulfilled we are equipped to deal with all the rest that life throws at us.

For us, the process of making is in itself simultaneously mindful meditation and an energy and mood enhancer. Making things is our therapy. We are happier, more resourceful and, hopefully, better people to be around. It is a state of mind and a way of being that we call 'craftfulness'. The same benefits for some are enjoyed through mindfulness and meditation, yoga, running, playing an instrument or singing, for example. The activity itself has wider benefits and implications for one's well-being and happiness, far beyond the object we have made or the race we have run. It has become integral to the pattern of our lives and led us to a rich community of encouraging, inspiring and collaborative fellow makers, many of whom, like us, have discovered additional well-being benefits through craft.

We are not craft experts. Neither one of us feels particularly 'artistic' in the conventionally perceived sense of the word; nor were we especially gifted students in art classes at school. We have day jobs as freelance editors that we love, but we are makers, menders, dabblers and gung-ho experimenters who are convinced of the mental health benefits of practising every day (or at least as often as is possible) a craft that inspires and challenges us. We are not neuroscientists advancing studies on brain chemistry or psychologists exploring the impact of a meditative practice on our mental health. But as experts on our own lives, we have very definite thoughts about why we make the things we do and why creativity and crafting is so important for our state of mind. In fact, we passionately believe that this matters more today than ever. For everyone.

In the following pages, we set out our manifesto for making and explain why we should all form a craft habit. As we will see, creating an object – from the idea to the finished work – is empowering, building confidence and resilience. Whether it's fulfilling an artistic urge or stitching something up that otherwise might be thrown away, it is a vital means of self-expression, self-realisation and self-help. Through making and mending things, we contend that you are also potentially making and mending yourself.

We share our personal experiences and insights as dedicated crafters, along with the stories of fellow makers who are pursuing practices that help them feel better about themselves, at home and at work, and who, like us, firmly believe that a regular craft activity makes a positive impact on their mental health.

In the process, we also investigate the areas of mindfulness, neuroscience, positive psychology and creativity research. And, while it is not our ambition to overwhelm you with countless research studies, we include salient or particularly interesting insights from the fields of science, medicine and contemporary social policy research where relevant. We visit vital and inspiring artistic community spaces and talk to GPs, psychologists, psychiatrists and experts in mental health care about the links between creative making and improved outcomes for well-being.

In **Part I**, we explore what we mean by creativity and discuss the importance of craft in our lives. We define our down-to-earth, *wabi-sabi*, craft ethos. A chapter on craft and mental health features an overview of the science and cites examples of the latest research and provides evidence that working with your hands in an active engagement with craft can have a huge impact on happiness.

In **Part II**, we tackle negativity, misconceptions and fears about creative ability and how to overcome obstacles by understanding what might be holding you back. We provide practical tips and suggestions on getting started and how to make time in a hectic life for everyday creative making. If you are new to craft, we suggest where you might find inspiration and which projects might be the right fit for you.

Part III provides short essays and some illustrated step-by-step guides for simple, yet inspiring, everyday craft projects to kick-start some ideas of your own or to add to your expanding craft repertoire.

***

What we have learned will hopefully inspire you to take up a new craft and start making. Or, if you are an established crafter you will already be aware of some of these benefits, but may not have named the release, the relief and the calm you feel when craft is part of your life.

This book is *not* about worshipping at the altar of the handmade, nor does it aim to repackage common sense into a zeitgeisty soundbite. We are not out to castigate, or dictate to anyone exactly how they spend their evenings and weekends. Nor do we want to imply that crafting solves everything. But, rather, to suggest ways of reintroducing balance into our lives and our habits; to encourage you to indulge in being creative for the sake of it, for the joy of doing and making exactly what you want; to suggest that reconnecting with that childhood state of *play* through craft will return more benefits than the piece of work we have knitted, sewed, drawn, thrown or woven. *Craftfulness* hopes to deliver the message that 'downtime' can also have a sense of purpose and deliver both the deep satisfaction enjoyed during the making process and the pleasure to be gained when the vision in your head becomes the object in your hands.

PART I

CHAPTER ONE

Craft and Creativity
(Or the life-changing magic of making things with your hands)

'In my spare time I want to do something "creative",
so I choose to do a bit of carpentering.'
– *George Orwell,* The Road to Wigan Pier

The idea of craft in itself may not mean very much to you if you've never had a creative hobby. For the uninclined it might conjure up unappealing images of childhood nursery activities, glitter glue and multicoloured pipe cleaners, the Girl Guides and Brownies badges, domestic science lessons, smocked nighties, crochet toilet-roll holders and sausage dog draught excluders.

We get it. In the not-too-distant past, crafts were consigned to fusty church hall bring-and-buy sales, twee gift shops and rural Christmas markets. Added to that cosy image there was, and to a certain extent still is, a huge amount of snobbery and condescension towards crafting from the art world – with a fair bit of misogyny thrown in. As amateur crafters, we have had to contend with certain stereotypes: that it's safe and simple and unthreatening; that it's mainly a female pursuit (for girls and women with too much time on their hands!); or that it's the domain of frustrated artists.

Thankfully, that narrative is being roundly challenged. Craft is on the rise, whether it's a more general celebration of the handmade or the increasing awareness that engaging head and hands to make something might make you feel better, as we will be discovering in this book. It's no longer seen as the armchair activity for empty nesters, the old or the lonely. For example, craft is being used increasingly to engage a socially and politically aware audience in ways that are original, challenging and persuasive – take the sight of a sea of pink handcrafted 'Pussyhats' descending on Washington, DC, in protest against Trump during January 2017's Women's March. The prejudices and norms of the art world are being challenged too by contemporary artists such as Freddie Robins, Celia Pym and Turner Prize-winning Grayson Perry, who combine traditional craft processes – knitting, darning, embroidery, weaving and pottery – with social commentary and political messages in their work.

We are currently living in a bright, new, exciting and disruptive age of craft. From traditional beers made in small breweries and artisan gins, to whole animal butcher shops and designer barbers, and from the explosion of global online craft and creativity retail outlets to social media platforms connecting crafters worldwide – craft is back with a bullet. You might say we are witnessing a twenty-first-century Arts and Crafts Movement.

The original Arts and Crafts Movement was inspired by the ideas of John Ruskin and William Morris in Britain around 1880. John Ruskin was a critic and theorist of the relationship between art, society and labour and William Morris was a socialist reformer, writer and designer who put Ruskin's philosophies into practice, placing great human value on work, the joy of traditional craft and the beauty of natural materials.

The Arts and Crafts Movement quickly spread to America and Europe before emerging finally as the *mingei* (folk crafts) movement in Japan. It was, in part, a reaction against the relentless force of capitalism and grew out of concerns about the brutalising face of the Industrial Revolution, which began in the second half of the eighteenth century: the dire conditions and dehumanising effects of large-scale mechanised factory labour. The Industrial Revolution uprooted the agricultural workforce – rural trades, traditional skills and handicrafts were no longer valued. The pace of life and very sense of natural, human time was transformed with the introduction of long factory hours and powered, special-purpose machinery, and the lives of ordinary working people changed forever.

Whereas in traditional craftsmanship, the skilled worker created alone a piece of fine, careful work, from start to finish, gaining purpose, pride, satisfaction and pleasure through his or her labour, the industrial model placed workers on manufacturing lines, making them responsible for single, monotonous, disjointed tasks. Central to Morris and Ruskin's philosophy was a yearning to retreat back to a more simple, slower-paced, rural life, a celebration of traditional crafts and the belief in the kinship of mankind and nature. Ironically, though, economic privilege proved a barrier for many then, as now, and for all Morris's noble socialist ideals, the new design ethos and pricey Arts and Crafts products were mainly only affordable to the wealthy.

Still, the Arts and Crafts Movement remains one of the most influential and visionary social movements of the modern age. And, as a model for a better way to live, work and value human labour, its basic principles seem acutely relevant today. There might be fewer of us working in factories these days, but with the rise of the technological and digital age, surely many of those original concerns and yearnings still resonate? The pace of our frenetic lives can sometimes feel overwhelming, as we try to balance our home lives with work, stay on top of the technology and social media overload, while struggling to keep perspective on what really matters to us. Inevitably, this is what is fuelling the resurgent thirst for the handmade. But also, in our opinion, there is an additional twenty-first-century malaise: our need and search for authenticity, meaning and a sense of control.

We live in a complex, random and often terrifying world in which, at times, it is easy to succumb to despair. Confronted by feelings of powerlessness, and without the balm of a religious faith or any strong political or social belief system to sustain us, many of us are seeking personal fulfilment, or at least something more meaningful.

Most of us no doubt daydream about opting out of the nine-to-five, of leading a more simple, less materialistic life pursuing an occupation closer to our hearts.

And if the return to a life in a little house on a distant prairie is unrealistic, we can at least strive to find a middle way. How can we make a living in a worthwhile endeavour that is not at the cost of others' well-being or our own? How can we make better, sustainable and more ethical choices? And how can we live a more balanced life with enough time to pursue those interests that matter to us, as we struggle to manage busy jobs that often spill over into our evenings and weekends?

However unpalatable the label, and whether we like it or not, we are consumers. And in that sense, one of the very few areas of our lives that we can control is our lifestyle choices: what we buy, what we eat, what we wear. For some it's the choice between local or supermarket honey, the handmade as opposed to the factory production line. We want meaning and authenticity in our consumption, for the human story behind the experience.

We find ourselves drawn to pastoral nostalgia, to credibility in material objects and in our life choices. This desire has been exploited somewhat by the handmade market, but, shopping weaknesses aside, it represents for us a new relationship with the *stuff* of our life.

Perhaps this is why there has been such a rise in crafting pursuits. Another, more direct and proactive way of countering feelings of powerlessness and lack of meaning is for you to become a maker, to take part in originating your own unique, handmade pieces.

MAKING STUFF AND HAPPINESS

'To make is to have a sense of yourself, a personal dignity which you can't get from consuming.'
– *Andrew Marr, A Short Book About Drawing*

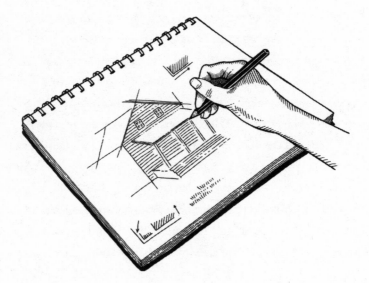

In the western world, we have largely lost touch with the body's facility for physical work. As the manufacturing and agricultural industries declined and the workplace became mechanised and later digitised, for so many of us work has become deskbound and the manual part of our jobs is often limited to using our fingers to type.

In *Happiness by Design*, Paul Dolan, Professor of Behavioural Science at the London School of Economics, discusses how we can all make it easier to be and feel happy, more of the time. But happiness is a highly subjective emotion – what makes one person ecstatic may send another screaming for the nearest exit. So, what exactly do we mean by it? Dolan makes a strong argument for the following: 'happiness is *experiences of pleasure and purpose over time*'.

Interestingly, this chimes with the Japanese concept of *ikigai*. Roughly translated, the word *ikigai* means 'a reason for being', a personal sense of 'what makes life worth living', from *iki*, meaning life, and *kai*, meaning the realisation of hopes and expectations. As in Dolan's definition of happiness found in the pursuit of goals seen as meaningful, *ikigai* incorporates positive feelings of pleasure with purpose over time. A sense of what makes life worthwhile need not be epic or grand in ambition in order to achieve maximum personal fulfilment and well-being. For some, their *ikigai* might be family, work or hobbies – this is pertinent because craft delivers *both pleasure and purpose* over time.

Well-being, Dolan says, is not about how you think, it's about what *you do*, and what you do with thoughts and feelings. We can adapt our mindset to pay less attention to issues that cause us emotional pain as part of consciously making changes in our behaviour and actions. In other words, we can be proactive in our search for happiness. We can deal with our thoughts differently: we can pay less attention to those that cause us grief; and we can take action to create opportunities and time for meaningful pursuits that add to personal happiness.

Working on a craft practice brings us pleasure because we choose to do crafts that we find relaxing and enjoyable. If we try a craft or technique and are not enjoying it, then we simply accept that woodturning, or linocuts, or crochet, is not for us, and stick to the activities that bring us joy. Craft is fulfilling because it has purpose – creating something with your own two hands is a meaningful and rewarding activity. So, when you devote some time every week or, even better, every day, to making, you are affording yourself more moments of happiness.

'I get a sense of achievement when I can use something I made. Seeing my bowls used in other people's homes is a source of the good kind of pride. I get to bring beauty into the world. That is a big thing. I feel that I have added something, that there is worth.'
– Katherine Kingsford, writer, potter

WE ARE CREATIVE BEINGS.
IT'S IN OUR GENES.

Creativity and happiness go hand in hand. But what is creativity exactly? At first glance, you might assume you know exactly what it means, it's obvious, isn't it? But when you try to define exactly what it is, it's a little trickier to pin down. An unscientific and random poll provided some very interesting results when people were asked the question, 'What does creativity mean to you?' Their short answers included a wide variety of instinctive responses: Toulouse-Lautrec in a smock with an easel and paint palette; Einstein; Beethoven; Virginia Woolf; Van Gogh; Picasso; Barbara Hepworth; John Lennon; clay; crayons; colour; daydreaming; hands; laughter; writing; clothes; magic; ideas; concentration; talking.

While, of course, creativity can mean many different things to different people, and definitions can vary according to the field of reference, we have a sense of the general direction of the term when we hear it. And, for the most part, we recognise creativity when we see it, whether it's an idea, a concept or an object that pulls us up short, turns our ideas around or inspires further research. Creativity in practice – in art, writing, advertising, fashion, design, technology or food – is something new, surprising, original, imaginative and fresh.

Here, in the context of 'craftfulness', our definition is pared back to the basics. Being creative for us is simply the act of making something, using your imagination and your hands as tools to express an idea or an emotion, by producing an object. It is also a mode of thinking differently: a creative mind allows you to form ideas for new ways of doing and to see the seemingly ordinary in a fresh light.

But if it's that simple, why is it that so many of our peers seem reluctant to describe themselves as 'creative'? Sir Ken Robinson is a world-renowned creativity expert who works within education systems and with governments and some of the world's leading cultural companies to unlock the creative energy of people and organisations. His book, *The Element: How Finding Your Passion Changes Everything*, describes the sense of finding your niche in a field where your natural talent blends perfectly with a personal passion.

As part of the research for his book, Robinson asks his audiences to rate their intelligence on a rising scale of 1 to 10, and then to likewise rate their creativity, then to raise their hand if they gave themselves different marks for intelligence and creativity: Intriguingly, typically between two-thirds and three-quarters of the audience raise their hands at this point, having usually rated their creativity at a significantly lower level. This, he argues, is one of the fundamental problems in our beliefs about creativity: that intelligence and creativity are very different qualities. We tend to think that we can be either one or the other. Robinson believes, however, that the highest form of intelligence is thinking creatively.

Many of us tend to equate creativity with creative genius, imagining figures such as Shakespeare or Picasso as the embodiment of the term. This exemplifies the myth that only very special people are creative or that only certain highbrow, distinguished activities are worthy of the authentic seal of creativity: the fine arts, classical music, fine opera and the theatre; or in the commercial world, the media, design, advertising or publishing, for example, might be viewed as creative industries. With mental references like these at play, it is not surprising that we might be reluctant to acknowledge our potential for creativity or boast of our unique imaginative talents.

Creative geniuses, however, are the exception rather than the rule. The paragons of the arts and sciences are blessed with what cognitive psychologists and creativity researchers Dr Mark A. Runco and Dr Ruth Richards identify as *eminent* creativity, a talent so highly refined that it earns their bearers a place in the history books. Whereas the opposite, 'everyday creativity', is exhibited by each of us every day as we decide which socks to wear or how to resolve issues at work.

In a nutshell, creativity is not confined to traditionally 'artistic' fields such as high culture, distinguished professions or the field of artisanal craftsmanship. You can be brilliantly creative as a plumber, footballer, hairdresser, PA, parent, teacher or whatever line of work you choose to pursue. As Robinson puts it, 'The fact is you can be creative in anything at all – anything that involves our intelligence.'

Possibly the most destructive myth is that you are born either naturally creative, or not at all (in Robinson's experiment you might be tempted to rate yourself a zero on the creativity scale!), that you might somehow have a more naturally artistic disposition or have inherited a creative gene, and that much like having green eyes and the ability to roll your *r*s — there's not much to be done about it.

This is not the case. Children are born with unlimited creative curiosity and imaginative powers. While many of us lose the free-flowing uninhibited creativity of our childhood, neuroscience now shows us that the brain is not a fixed and static organ. We can exercise our brain to build different neural pathways to strengthen certain areas or work on weaknesses in the same way we would train for a triathlon. Whatever your age, background or education, you *can* become more creative in your life and work. In the same way you might exercise to build certain muscles, brain-training exercises will isolate and focus on areas you wish to develop, such as improving memory, problem solving, learning and concentrating attention.

Therefore, if everyone has innate creative capacity, then your belief system about talent or natural ability isn't really relevant. Everyone can express their creativity by making. As we'll explore in more depth in **Part II**, it doesn't really matter at all if you don't create a perfect artwork or object at first, because it's the flexing of your creative muscle that counts: the real 'value' is not necessarily in the outcome, the finished piece, but in pursuing your creative impulse.

When you find pleasure and relaxation in a craft activity that is right for you, whether it's cooking, or gardening, or in a craft as a knitter, embroiderer, bookbinder, potter, etc., you are eminently, joyfully creative.

In *Making Is Connecting*, David Gauntlett's definition of creativity is pleasingly user-friendly: 'Everyday creativity refers to a process which brings together at least one active human mind, and the material or digital world, in the activity of making something which is novel.' Gauntlett's creativity is, in essence, about new directions and new experiences, trying something that you've never done before, or doing it differently. He says 'creativity might be better understood as a *process*, and a *feeling*'.

So, for all the definitions and quality control caveats, when you break it down and accept everyday creativity as a feeling, a process – a joyful state of being that we can actively flex and foster – creativity is really not at all elusive or unattainable.

CREATIVITY AS COMMODITY – WHY CREATIVITY IS MORE IMPORTANT THAN EVER BEFORE

With the exception perhaps of 'creative accounting', it is universally agreed that creativity is a positive force, an enviable and precious human gift. We can be creative in our lives in much the same way that we are with our making projects. We can take risks, work hard and consider the opportunities that come our way more thoughtfully. Our lives can become the canvas against which the decisions we make paint a picture of a life fully explored.

Today creativity has become an increasingly valuable commodity. In fact, according to many leading thinkers in business, creativity *is* the future. In *A Whole New Mind: Why Right-Brainers Will Rule the Future*, Daniel Pink, one of our leading business thinkers, writes that 'right brain' traits such as emotional intelligence, exuberance, empathy, intuition and original thinking – all characteristics of creative personality types – will become increasingly important in determining 'who flourishes and who founders' in the workplace.

Raise your hand if at work you've been subjected to a Creative Leadership course or attended a meeting where 'thought showers' and 'creative brainstorming' topped the agenda. The problem with these approaches is that leadership training, team away days, blue-sky-thinking sessions and 'big ideas' meetings are often a sure-fire way to dull the brain of even the most creative genius in the room. Great pressure or even the best-meaning exhortations to be imaginative can have the opposite effect – and this is especially true in the workplace. In our experience, whenever we were on the receiving end of demands to be spontaneously innovative, our reaction certainly was to instantly clam up – it felt like we had not a single molecule of imagination nor a creative cell in our entire bodies.

We're not disparaging the efforts that corporations make to energise their staff. Inspiring the workforce to be happier and more creative is a forward-thinking approach in business, but we feel that the methods often miss their mark, and can sometimes have the impact of adding stress to an already overburdened workload.

There are many ways to empower employees, but one direction we found especially interesting was from the team behind the 64 Million Artists initiative. A national campaign to unlock people's potential through everyday creativity, 64 Million Artists has as its premise that you don't have to be an artist to be creative. Founder Jo Hunter visited workplaces and ran workshops with employees centred around the idea of reconnecting with their personal artistic passions. Staff were allowed a half-day off every month to explore their areas of interest, some of which included drawing and painting, planning one's own funeral and, notably, one woman taught all the men in her family a dance for her wedding! The results were fascinating: companies heralded it as transformative; employees were engaged, inspired and found a new energy for the pastime of their choice. They reported feeling more motivated at work and because they shared the results of their creativity with their workmates, felt a greater bond. How can this fail to have a positive impact on a company as a whole?

Big ideas tend to appear when we are least expecting or prepared for them – and often when we are not striving for solutions, not actively doing, but rather when we allow the mind to wander. You might find inspiration while staring at teabags in the supermarket, cleaning the bath, knitting, bookbinding, sewing, mending or weaving on a mini-loom – craft helps us to slow down, to relax and breathe. With knitting, for example, the rhythm of regular repeated stitches has an almost hypnotic effect. Thoughts quieten and, while the active brain is focused on the task at hand, the untethered resting mind can wander, to expand and explore deeper realms of the unconscious, and sometimes spark new ideas and new ways of looking at old issues.

The benefits of a regular craft practice do not cease having an impact the second you put down your tools and head off to the day job either. We have found that our making has made us much more self-assured and creative in every part of our lives, more awake and contented. After a morning spent in the pottery studio, Rosemary knows now that she returns to editing a tricky passage in a manuscript with more zip and positive energy – it's as though the batteries have been fully charged while she was working on the clay coils. Arzu loves losing herself in her bookbinding – the attention that is required when working on the file detail is all enveloping. To make a good book, one must fold, crease, cut, sew, bind and press with care. This takes time, but is intensely satisfying. And usually, before the last book is removed from the press, she has always found that new ideas will already be starting to take shape.

As we will see throughout this book, once creativity is awakened it has a tangible impact on the rest of your life, of that there is little doubt in terms of scientific research and anecdotally via fellow makers quoted in *Craftfulness*.

'Craftfulness' is about embracing creative potential to come up with different ways of solving problems or facing life's challenges, while giving us a stillness of mind that allows these issues to bubble up to the surface in a way that is constructive and helpful. As we will see later, it encourages a flexibility in our thinking: we feel more comfortable dealing with confusion, conflicts or change. Creativity means we can challenge the systems, envision alternative ways of managing our lives, avoid group and corporate thinking and approach our work life with new confidence and vim. It is no exaggeration to say that if you find yourself in a position where you need to make a big life change such as a career move, the inner confidence you have gained from pursuing a 'craftfulness' practice can help you steer that course too. Trust us, we've been there.

We weren't being flippant when we said it took creativity to choose the right socks to wear in the morning. It might not always feel so, but we are making tiny creative decisions as we go about our lives every single day. James C. Kaufman, Professor of Educational Psychology at the University of Connecticut, is a psychologist and researcher known for his work with Dr Ronald A. Beghetto on their Four C model of creativity.

According to this model, *mini-c* is concerned with deliberate creativity, such as painting a picture or beginning a craft project, while *Pro-c* is where we make a living from our creative pursuits, as an artist or a designer, for example. Then there's *Big-C* or Eminent Creativity, which is where one enters the history books because of a profound and creative contribution, such as from the likes of Ada Lovelace or Albert Einstein.

Finally, there's *little-c*. This is the one we're particularly interested in. This is everyday creativity, which is simply 'originality brought to tasks in everyday life'. It isn't just about artistic expression, however; as illustrated above, it is a quality we bring to all aspects of our lives – how we approach problems and resolve them, how we raise a young family and manage our jobs. All of us engage in routine everyday creativity – it's a fact. If you've ever decorated your house, put on make-up, got a tattoo, daydreamed, made a list of priorities, fixed the taps in the bathroom or tried a new recipe – then you have proved the theory. If we believe creativity is about problem solving and adapting our environment to suit our needs, then we are all creative. Everyday creativity is part of being human, a natural impulse to work around obstacles, make do and mend where necessary.

Once you accept that not everyone needs to be a Ms Grace Hopper or a Mr James Dyson or even Bob Marley, then it's just a small step to developing a habit that puts *mini-c* into bat – deliberate, regular, creative activities that require little or no expert knowledge – which in *Craftfulness* means developing a craft habit.

CHAPTER TWO

Our Craft Ethos
(It's the making that matters)

- -

'I keep a diary that is part writing and part drawing.
While I am drawing I feel self-conscious when I start,
but very soon the floodgates open and I lose
myself in the process.'
— *Lisa Gornick, filmmaker, drawing*

Central to the ethos of 'craftfulness' is the idea that the act of
making is where the magic happens. The sense of pleasure and
purpose when working on a project gives craft its meaning.
Hand in hand with the tremendous enjoyment in the moment
when absorbed in a craft process that we love is the added bonus
of seeing the object of our imagination grow, evolve, take form
and come into being. The slow, steady, incremental results of our
labour serve the function of a reward.

We have yet to meet a crafter who finds their pastime
burdensome, or who feels reluctance at the idea of returning
to it day after day.

But, crucially, it must be *your* choice and *your* interests that dictate your course. Any task that you are compelled to do by an outside force, be it at work or in school, is unlikely to be as joyful or pleasurable as something that inspires and excites you and that you have embarked on purely for your own personal enjoyment.

Of course, crafting is not for everyone, but everyone can benefit from periods of intense concentration on an inspiring project or activity. It is important to respond to your instincts and if they dictate birdwatching, baking or badminton, take heed! Arzu likes crochet; Rosemary can't get the hang of it and doesn't see the point. Why crochet, she asks, when you can knit? Arzu concurs. Each to their own. Don't stress and only do what you enjoy.

Bringing your awareness to the present moment through mindful meditation, and through any focused activity in which you are alert to what is happening right now, has been shown to regulate mood, reduce stress and anxiety and improve sleeping patterns.

A mindful state is where you notice your thoughts, see your actions, but are not compelled to engage with them. You become an impartial observer of what is playing out in your head, whereas before your thoughts may have aroused paralysing negative feelings and self-judgement. The space between thinking and observing your thoughts is where the work happens.

Practising mindfulness can help us deal with difficult issues in our lives. We might ask, is worrying about this problem useful? Are these negative and repetitive thoughts getting in the way of seeing the problem for what it is? The intention is not to dispel these uncertainties entirely, but rather to see them as *separate* from ourselves, recognise that they are just thoughts. Whether it's a recent falling-out with a friend or negative feedback from a work colleague, excessive preoccupation with events we can do nothing to alter is only going to jeopardise our forward momentum.

Whichever technique you use, be it a daily meditation, yoga or just bringing your awareness back to your body whenever you feel fraught and distracted, mindfulness is a valuable tool for negotiating our increasingly frenetic lives. It is not the magic pill to instantly harmonise all aspects of our experience, rather, it helps us to interrogate whether the problems on which we endlessly ruminate are as bad or as distracting as all the headspace we devote to them. Some thoughts, of course, are a normal response to our reality, and to suppress them is unhealthy – but it's what we decide to do with them, and how to act on them, that counts. Occasionally, time away from a problem provides the valuable detachment needed to come back to our issues with fresh eyes and new ideas.

Our craft activity performs a similar mindful function to meditation: when Rosemary is knitting and Arzu is preparing her Japanese woodblock prints, awareness of the outside world is reduced, the volume turned down, while attention and focus remain exclusively on the project itself. This intense concentration (or *flow* state – more on which later in Chapter Four) has similar neurological effects on the brain as meditation. In our craft pursuits we are focused, absorbed in the task at hand, aware of a profound sense of satisfaction.

'When I'm in the pottery studio I have a pronounced sense of calm, I feel at once practical, peaceful and very lucky. The joy of working to my own pace is important to me. Much of my working life is tightly scheduled and, as a Londoner, I move at the pace the city requires of me. I arrive at pottery out of breath, full of the day's anxieties. Very quickly I feel my shoulders drop, my breath slows, my body feels different and issues at work or in life that felt insurmountable seem smaller and more manageable, pushed to the back of my mind. Even when my lesson is over or I've left the studio, the earlier problem seems halved, or at least far less troubling. Is my subconscious working it out or at least putting it in perspective, while I'm concentrating completely on centring a bowl or glazing a plate? Or perhaps there's something more primal at work. I am making something with my own hands, working on a piece that will be useful and practical and with a process that is more all-encompassing and important than an unfinished email or a tricky conversation from earlier in the day.'
— *Chloe Healy, marketing director, potter*

We know the value of craft in our lives and so do countless other crafters. We are drawn to the regular periods set aside to make our work. We may not have knowingly recognised it as a well-being exercise, but we intrinsically know the function of it. If we're not making, then something is out of kilter. There may be periods when we're not as focused as we'd like to be, life intrudes and our routine drops off, but we always return to it. None of this is news, but what is interesting is the fact that craft is increasingly cited by health professionals and academics as one way of easing certain mental health issues such as chronic pain and depression, as we will see in Part II.

'Drawing gets me out of myself, it's like meditating, it relaxes me, it's like a lovely drug. I draw with ink, not pencil and whatever comes out, comes out. The drawing is an imprint of my brain.'
— *Lisa Gornick, filmmaker, drawing*

USING OUR HANDS

'I encourage everyone to use their hands. Process is so important, hands connecting with the mind, it is a terrific well-being pursuit.'
— *Freddie Robins, senior tutor for knitted textiles, Royal College of Art, London*

Darian Leader writes provocatively about our basic need to use our hands as a fundamental, healthy expression of desire and drive. In his intriguing book *Hands: What We Do with Them – and Why*, Leader argues that we *have to* use our hands; it's a natural compulsion. We fidget, mould, knead, shape, pick, pluck and touch. We feel compelled to keep them busy and to make things.

We also use our hands to communicate through gesture and to express ourselves through art. Our hands are linked to the part of our brain we use for language – it's almost impossible not to wave our hands around while we talk, or even while we listen to others talking to us. Indeed, Anna Freud, when asked what a psychoanalyst should do when listening to a patient in therapy, recommended not note-taking, as you might expect, but knitting.

Making things with your hands is an instinctive, ancient form of self-expression, a powerful language in material form. It is ultimately more satisfying than watching TV or obsessively checking Twitter and Instagram feeds (addictive though that might be).

Our ancestors used their hands for survival, whether it was building shelters or setting traps to catch their food and then preparing it or, in the more recent past, to spin, weave, sew and knit for clothing or to milk, churn, mill and grind to make raw ingredients – fulfilling basic needs that today we take for granted. The labour of supplying the basics of daily life – food, shelter, protection, clothing, warmth – was not simply physical work, however – these manual tasks require intricate thought processes.

Most of us are no longer required to knit our children's leggings, weave tabards or even peel and chop our own potatoes to make chips. In the late 1990s, Kelly Lambert, behavioural scientist and author of *Lifting Depression*, began thinking about the impact our contemporary lifestyle has on mental health. Given that the lives of our grandparents were tougher, why, she wonders, is the incidence of depression ten times higher for people born in the latter part of the twentieth century?

Lambert's study asks if our mental health suffered when we swapped ploughing fields for trawling the internet. Of course, neither we nor Lambert are advocating a return to the homestead: Lambert explains that our brains are hardwired to respond positively to physical exertion by rewarding us with deep satisfaction when our labours produce tangible results.

Using data culled from MRI scans tracking brain activity during different tasks, Lambert found that physical labour influenced well-being. Labelling it the 'effort-driven reward circuit', she found that the areas of the brain associated with reward, emotion, movement and higher reasoning were connected.

Effort-driven reward is an evolutionary tool to ensure the survival of the species. Physical work not only brings a sense of emotional well-being when we see the positive results of our efforts, but also makes us feel more in control of our surroundings and ultimately helps us to build resilience to mental illness, such as depression.

In one other fascinating experiment, Lambert observed two groups of rats, where Group A had to dig for the reward of a treat, while Group B enjoyed 'free' treats. Six weeks later, each rat was presented with an unsolvable problem. The digger rats, Group A, persisted at the problem nearly twice as long as the non-diggers. Lambert concluded that the rats that had to work for their treats were immunised against the 'learned helplessness' often associated with depression.

When the effort-driven reward circuit is activated in our brains, the greater our sense of well-being and the more positive we feel. Meaningful goal-driven physical activity encourages these neural connections, important for combatting depression. When we use both body (the hands) and mind, we enjoy a fuller brain experience than in purely intellectual-driven reward, and this helps prepare us for life's next challenge.

As we have lost the requirement for movement, the brain is not engaged in the way it was designed to function. Fewer and fewer of us are employed in manual physical labour, and so our opportunity to experience the specific brain activation associated with effort-driven reward has diminished. The negative side-effect is a loss of our sense of control over our environment, making us vulnerable to mental health problems.

One way to counteract this, especially if your work is intensely mind- and thought-driven, is to use your hands to start making. Of course, throwing a pot or weaving on a loom is no longer necessary for the survival of the species, but given that the brain's neural pathways behave in the same way whether we are churning butter or performing intricate heart surgery, the important point is that the effort-driven reward system is stimulated in the same way. Lambert argues convincingly that this process is important for our mental health, because making things makes us feel effective.

Using our hands to think about a problem, such as cleaning, mending, cooking, knitting or gardening, where the end goal is meaningful, is like taking a mental health vitamin, Lambert concludes. Any useful task that engages your hands gives you a sense of control over your environment and is, ultimately, very empowering. Craftwork brings exactly the same brain rewards.

'In my twenties, I was finishing a medical degree but had very mixed feelings about doctoring, so I spent ten years looking for the creative counterpoint to this, building theatre sets, training in cabinetmaking and doing a year's apprenticeship in furniture-making. In work terms, that was the best year of my life: a perfect match of someone hungry to learn, with a huge new palette of tools to work with in a wood workshop. That was the year making became obsessional for me, like an ecstasy. I wanted to work eighteen-hour days, and do nothing else. It was like an intoxicating mixture of play and work, and the very best aspect of work: that which absorbs one completely, where you acquire skills, and where you have an invested ownership of the outcome. It invited mental problem solving that naturally opened a part of my brain that delighted in being unlocked. The motivation in sticking with my woodwork and making is probably some attempt to recreate that time, to hold on to that intensity of engagement. And now, it's how not to burnout, go nuts as a GP. To enjoy life and hold on to the part of my brain that is stimulated in the process of working with wood.'

– Will Brook, GP, woodworking

CHAPTER THREE

Craft, Creativity & Mental Health

(Making is mending)

'I had learned to crochet as a child, but I had never done
more than the basics. About ten years ago, in my late
twenties, I was going through a period of deep depression,
and I was grasping at straws for anything that would make
me feel better. I read somewhere that you should do what
you loved to do as a child and for some reason crochet
came to mind so I decided to give it a try again. It helped
immediately, and I've been crocheting regularly ever since.'
— *Kathryn Vercillo, writer, crocheting*

Many of us at some point in our lives may experience mild to
moderate symptoms of depression, including sadness, indifference
or lack of motivation, low self-esteem, poor concentration and low
energy. Grief and sadness brought on by loss and bereavement, or
fear of upheaval and anxiety about what the future holds, can feel
overwhelming at times and may affect our ability to cope. Intense

feelings such as these are part of being human and as such can be termed human condition ailments.

Environmental factors and external pressures of modern life play a part in our mental health, with increasing numbers of people, including teenagers and students, citing symptoms of stress and debilitating anxiety. Excessive worrying, rumination, insomnia and irritability can have a chronic effect on well-being, thwarting our ability to function and thrive.

'Self-help' gets a bit of a bad rap, but essentially it is about making certain choices to improve our health and well-being – who among us can claim that they wouldn't benefit from some self-initiated tweaks? Eating well, exercising and getting enough sleep form the basic toolkit for happiness. But exploring our creativity, our capacity to inspire and be inspired, to use our hands to make objects which express our innate individuality are also to be cherished and encouraged.

We know from personal experience that some form of creative activity has proved essential to our happiness and mental health. Our conversations around Rosemary's kitchen table or in Arzu's garden often took place during periods of stress. Full-time jobs and the demands of children can lead to burnout; certainly when your children are very young it can feel as though one is always on high alert, always on the edge of a crisis, whether it's managing childcare or juggling a work emergency.

Rosemary herself has struggled with depression and bipolar disorder since her late teens and, during her worst breakdowns and periods off work, found that knitting, along with word puzzles and TV quiz shows, was one of the very few things that she could continue to do, and that brought any respite from the debilitating mental pain. The act of knitting, its repetitive rhythm, calms and soothes. While hands and mind are engaged with the knitting in your lap, watching the rows growing in repeating patterns takes some of the pain away. Now, she finds that working with clay and hand-building with coils has the same sedative effect.

That said, having always had the drive to make things, it was only relatively recently that we began to properly think about the role of craft in our lives and to analyse the deeply therapeutic part it played. Making made us feel better, cope better, engage more fully with the world around us, feel inspired and useful.

The actual process of being creative and of making things with our hands, we now recognise, is in itself the incidental and fundamental mental health benefit. Through 'craftfulness' we can all tap into this innate creative potential.

CREATIVITY IS THE ORIGINAL ANTI-DEPRESSANT

'Man is most nearly himself when he achieves the seriousness of a child at play.'
– *Heraclitus, 500 BCE, philosopher*

Creativity is an intrinsic part of our human-ness – homo sapiens' ability to imagine and think and to relate thought in symbolic form – language, art forms, writing – distinguishes us from every other species. It is interesting to note within this context that we evolved to use our hands to create objects of artistic, emotional and symbolic expression.

In *Arts in Health*, research scientist Daisy Fancourt presents a compelling and inspiring history of art and creativity in medicine and psychiatric health, as well as demonstrates the positive impact and well-being potential of the arts. Fancourt points out that the earliest traces of our creativity can be seen in Palaeolithic cave paintings, thought to be prehistoric examples of symbolic expression relating to health. She notes that the earliest pieces of art, dated to around 40,000 years ago, are thought to have been part of ancient healing and fertility rituals.

Today, the growing body of research from clinical trials leaves little room for doubt that creative activity in which people participate because they want to, in an unpressured environment, delivers therapeutic benefits that are positive, significant and can be life-changing. Indeed, in his book *Creativity as Repair: Bipolarity and its Closure*, Andrew Brink of the department of Psychiatry at McMaster University makes the plain and bold assertion that creativity is the 'original anti-depressant'.

While it would be irresponsible to claim that 'craftfulness' and creativity alone can cure all – severe and chronic mental health illnesses, including bipolar disorders and schizophrenia, call for prescribed clinical and drug treatment plans – it does bear noting that even in these more serious incidents of mental health crises, as in Rosemary's experience, creative engagement, as part of a complementary, holistic therapeutic approach may play a vital role in the healing programme.

We spoke with the Bound by Veterans charity (formerly the Wiltshire Barn Project), which was founded in 2012 by two bookbinders who shared the strong belief that this craft could be of therapeutic benefit to wounded, injured and sick ex-servicemen and women. The courses run by the charity aim to give veterans, or individuals being discharged from the services, the opportunities to enjoy not just the well-being benefits of bookbinding, but also to attain internationally recognised qualifications in the book arts.

For many servicemen and women who suffer severe physical and mental injuries including post-traumatic stress disorder (PTSD) and depression, bookbinding provides a set of skills which aren't too demanding, and which produce simple, yet unique books and boxes at the end of the course. This gives the maker a great sense of achievement and satisfaction. Binding books is a craft where one is always learning: it is an ideal craft for therapy, in that it is possible to make simple books with very basic skills in a short time; however, over longer periods, structures with increasing complexity are equally satisfying. The feedback from attendees is overwhelmingly positive; those who have endured great physical and mental stress find relief in the simple process of putting together books and making boxes.

A RAF senior non-commissioned officer with over 20 years' service shared his thoughts with us: 'Taking the course has helped me tremendously. I was unable to get out of the house for eight months, except for medical appointments, and too nervous to drive anywhere. I now enjoy the journey to the Barn for work. I feel more stable and not so anxious about the future. I'm so busy concentrating on the work, cutting and stitching or making marbled paper, that everything else is pushed to one side.'

Some veterans found their short-term memories dramatically affected by the medication required subsequent to their injuries. Bound by Veterans' founder Jonathan Powell highlights the power of bookbinding to aid short-term memory recovery: 'Everything we do requires a little bit of imagination, a lot of concentration and an increasingly well-developed memory. Going through routines is very repetitive but beneficial. It's good for short-term memory as you have to remember stages and processes. There is a tremendous boost in confidence if you get it right and end up with a functional object. The veterans want it to be perfect and when it is, there's nothing like the feeling.'

You can get a taste of this yourself in **Part III**, where you can try your hand at putting a book together.

One of the most inspiring and uplifting places we visited in the course of our research is Core Arts in Hackney, London. Founder and artist Paul Monks showed us around the building, a restored church hall just off Chatsworth Road near Hackney's Homerton Hospital, housing a vast gallery showing some of the clients'

extraordinary work, recording and rehearsal studios, a fully
equipped pottery, painting and life-drawing rooms and digital
media suites. Paul told us how Core Arts started. In the early
1990s, he was using vacant space in the old Hackney Hospital
to paint. Curious patients, seeking respite from the monotony
of their day on the psychiatric ward, soon chanced upon his
studio door. Paul invited them in. Before long, he had a growing
number of regular visitors and his studio became a haven for
artistic expression, as patients sought refuge from the clinical
setting in a world of paint and colour.

'These guys would just come in and sit and chat while I was
painting. I had a massive industrial box of paint, so I invited
them to have a go, and it just grew from that. I thought hard
about the myth of creativity and mental health. I found out that
many of my visitors were doing creative things on their own, in
their own way. I wasn't privy to those experiences, so I started
visiting them in their flats and saw amazing sights. I saw people
who had nothing but a candle and a can of Guinness, who
painted the walls, or plastered them making 3D images. I saw
this chap who had literally 40,000 rap poems, stacked up in piles
of paper, they were just bits of paper he'd found and written on,
these fantastic raps, and that's all he was doing.'

It became clear to Monks that time and again psychiatric
patients were being discharged into the community and left
to their own devices. There was no capacity to engage these
patients and often the patients themselves didn't know what to
ask for. Paul learned that by asking the question, 'What do you

do?' Listening to the answer, he could begin to provide a positive response to it in the form of the opportunity and a setting for creative expression that so many so desperately needed. 'We started to get spaces and materials and people attended because they *wanted* to.'

Twenty-six years on, Core Arts is a vibrant community space offering over eighty creative classes a week, in which clients and their tutors are equally engaged in a learning and creative process and enabling people who experience mental health issues to overcome barriers, fulfil their potential and participate fully in their community. Paul says, 'The interesting thing about craft activity when I talk to some of the tutors is that so many of them are just happy with the process or the journey – this is key.'

'I haven't been able to work full-time for more than a decade. I went to drama school and have worked as an actor, theatre practitioner and playwright but I suffered a breakdown in my twenties as a result of my undiagnosed autism – it was eventually diagnosed when I was thirty-two. I started doing pottery as an after-school activity when I was a child. I was good at it and enjoyed it. At one time I was so keen I went twice a week. When I had a nervous breakdown I went to my mother's and hid from the world for a while. My family had read about art therapy and thought doing some pottery might help me so they contacted my old pottery teacher and obtained some supplies and helped me get a kiln. I began making twisted trees out of clay. The feeling of the soft, wet malleability, the sense of partnership with the desired shape, drawing it out; it gave me some focus and purpose. I couldn't write at that time, my brain hurt. Clay sculpture does not require much conscious thought.

Hands talk to the clay, a dialogue without words, and the eye guides, but hard thinking is not required. It kept me occupied and focused while my mind healed. It is an artistic and creative outlet very different from writing. I am much better now, busy and more fulfilled, but when

I was ill it helped to fill the dead time. It gave me a purpose when I badly needed one, something to focus on that had tangible and useful results. It is a productive way to enjoy myself. And it's fun.'

– Katherine Kingsford, writer, potter

'I think my motivation to craft mainly came from both my mother and sister. We actively encouraged an interest in each other for what we were doing and were able to exchange thoughts and ideas, which gave each of us a real sense of pleasure and achievement. When my sister died I think I initially made a conscious decision to quilt less – perhaps I felt it was something we shared together and felt it was wrong to do it without her. However, that feeling did pass to be replaced by a desire to sew and quilt as I used to, so that in some way I was carrying on doing what she loved and what we shared together and our shared memories. I still visit shows but prefer to go on my own even though friends offer to accompany me – that time on my own gives me space to reflect on what my sister and I would have shared together and to feel close to her.'

— *Pauline Smith, retired teacher, quilter*

When we visited Art House Sheffield, an inspiring creative learning space and mental health social enterprise, the ceramics teacher, Sarah Vanic, showed us around the inspiring pottery studio as she explained: 'Creativity is a crucial function. People can often survive terrible events and excruciating circumstances because they take themselves somewhere else in their minds. Our minds are boundary-less. There is a parallel with making – there doesn't have to be boundaries unless you impose them on your project.'

Although limited research has been carried out specifically on crafting and well-being, neuroscientists are beginning to recognise that studies that focus on cognitive ability activities, such as completing word puzzles, might also apply to complex crafts such as quilting, knitting or embroidery.

Quoted in a recent CNN article, Catherine Carey Levisay, a clinical neuropsychologist and wife of **Craftsy.com** CEO John Levisay, says, 'There's promising evidence coming out to support what a lot of crafters have known anecdotally for quite some time. Creating – whether it be through art, music, cooking, quilting, sewing, drawing, photography (or) cake decorating – is beneficial to us in a number of important ways.'

CREATIVITY, CRAFT AND A
HEALTHY SENSE OF SELF

'I make crafting a priority because I believe it is critical
to my mental health. I typically set aside time each day to
craft. I work from home so it's something that I can
easily do on breaks between writing.'
— Kathryn Vercillo, writer, crocheting

D. W. Winnicott, influential paediatrician and psychologist, worked extensively on the role of play for children. Winnicott focused on the child's development of a sense of self as separate from the parent. He proposed that we evolve a sense of identity and form strategies for understanding and adapting to our place within the family and the wider world through creative play in childhood.

By separating from the parent, Winnicott asserted, we form an awareness of our own inner urges and impulses and become individuals with our own authentic identity, and we become our true selves. But in order to fit in and not be rejected, this *true self* must occasionally be masked or suppressed, and the child must form an 'alternative self' to present to the world which Winnicott termed the *false self.*

This other face is a necessary evil in that it allows us to interact and become social beings, but our *true self* must find expression and guide our behaviour for the majority of the time to maintain a healthy psyche. It's really all about balance; if we spend too much time hiding our *true self* and bury our most basic feelings and impulses, then we lose part of who we are, our authentic personality.

Although depression and anxiety, the most common forms of mental illness, can have a biological component, arising from chemical imbalance, these conditions can also be triggered or exacerbated by unconscious conflict caused by negative experiences such as childhood neglect and deprivation, trauma, early loss of a parent or sibling, poverty and social isolation and other painful life events.

When we are being creative and making, and if we allow the mind to roam undirected and unmoored, we tap into our unconscious thoughts and reconnect with Winnicott's *authentic self*. This, in turn, can lead to moments of real insight and a happy awakening or lifting of emotions. Freud wrote about 'ordinary unhappiness', such as the human condition ailments referred to on p. 34, but he was also convinced that artistic, intellectual and psychological work can increase pleasure and create joy.

Crafting connects the mind and the body in what amounts to a deeply therapeutic process. By establishing mindfulness and 'craftfulness' techniques, we allow ourselves to experience intense or challenging emotions without the accompanying self-judgement or the need to censor painful memories.

Sarah Vanic stresses that mindful craft has qualities that are unique. 'Using your creativity can maintain health and well-being, foster imagination and make a space for the reverie you can feel when you are making.'

If we acknowledge, tend to and accept our inner life, we can accept and better deal with issues such as low self-esteem, which are holding us back and making us ill, and build appropriate coping responses. When we begin to make and build pride in our practical ability, we may also start to uncover untapped reserves of inner joy, strength, resilience and talent. A sense of competence and self-reliance encourages greater control of our lives and with that control the world may feel less daunting. Whatever challenges life throws at you, you are better able to meet them face-on and stay standing: you have got the tools to shield and save yourself. You are a warrior armed only with Japanese woodblock tools, knitting needles and a crochet hook!

If you can do that and see it through to the end, what else can you do? Cope with? Make a start on?

'My mum not only taught me to knit, but also to sew and bake. I spent hours tending to these crafts largely for their meditative effects. Fast forward to adulthood, I found myself completely disillusioned with my career as a lawyer and left to work in my husband's fashion retail business. Three children then came along in fairly quick succession and I stopped work for full-time parenting. I was totally unprepared for how difficult mothering can be. Postnatal depression took a hold of me and I felt like a failure.

'I certainly sought medical and professional help for my mental health issues and that was important to my recovery, but it wasn't until I started knitting again in 2010 that my life started turning around. I have completely transformed my life and my outlook and it all comes down to living a creative life. I had lived most of my life in denial of my creative self and as a result I completely lost my way. I was a sitting duck for depression. I have always loved working with my hands but now it's more important than ever as it is essentially a critical part of maintaining a healthy and happy emotional life. That's a huge motivating force.

'Mental illness affects an extraordinary amount of people from all walks of life and it is often the most sensitive and creative amongst us that find themselves in its grips. Since delving into the world of wool and knitting I have found solace, peace, joy, affirmation and mindfulness. I no longer suffer from depression and manage my anxiety as well as anyone else.'

— Jacqui Fink, extreme knitter, fibre artist

DREAMING, DOODLING AND NOODLING –
LET YOUR MIND WANDER …

For a good portion of any day, we are bombarded with external forms of stimulation that require *directed*, as opposed to *undirected* thinking. Directed thinking requires that we concentrate our focus on a particular task or conundrum, whereas undirected thinking is neither coherent nor goal-oriented, but allows the mind to wander, as in dreaming and daydreaming.

Unfortunately, our hectic and time-pressured lives rarely provide the space for a roving mind. Modern technology and digital forms of communication call for seemingly continual directed thinking – we are inundated with emails, texts, Snapchats; each ping on our device demanding instant attention and response. We worry about wasting time, yet pore over articles on productivity, time management and super-achievers' effectiveness tips. Perhaps, being busy all the time, not thinking too deeply or letting the mind wander, are defence mechanisms – don't think, just keep going, block out troubling feelings that might be bubbling under the surface of a seemingly organised and ordered life.

In 2010, a LexisNexis survey of 1,700 white-collar workers in the United States, the UK, Australia, China and South Africa revealed that, on average, employees spent more than half their workdays receiving, responding to and organising their emails, rather than using the information conveyed within to do their jobs.

But studies indicate that undirected thinking is vital for creativity, productivity and, most importantly, our mental health. Sonja Lyubomirsky, Professor of Psychology at the University of California and author of *The How of Happiness*, suggests that periods of mental time out are necessary for us to flourish, or as the Alexander Technique teaches to 'not do', but instead to occasionally 'just be'. Downtime, it seems, is as essential to the brain as healthy food and regular exercise are to our bodies.

When we are absorbed in the process of making, our minds rest and roam. Feelings and ideas that might otherwise be blocked or drowned out by the demands of directed thinking take root and hopefully inspire new ideas, projects and creations.

Research shows that even when we are relaxing or daydreaming, the brain is anything but idle. Downtime replenishes the brain's stores of attention and motivation, and encourages productivity and creativity. Research also indicates that any number of activities where the brain and the hand connect in absorbing and deliberate, repetitive, focused movements (such as in knitting, weaving, sewing, even chopping vegetables) can be useful for diffusing stress and distracting the mind from unhelpful rumination and negative thinking loops.

When we give our minds a break, areas of the brain are in fact hard at work relieving the negative effects of stress, restoring our creative energies and forming new memories and connections essential for our sense of self and mental health. The complex circuit at work when we enter an unfocused resting state is known as the default mode network (DMN). In a review of research in 2012 on the default mode network, Mary Helen Immordino-Yang of the University of Southern California and her co-authors write: 'Downtime is an opportunity for the brain to surface fundamental unresolved tensions in our lives ... [to] mull over the aspects of our lives with which we are most dissatisfied, searching for solutions [...] These moments of introspection are also one way we form a sense of self, which is essentially a story we continually tell ourselves.'

Making things, therefore, gives our overactive brain a much-needed break, and some unpressured time to tap into intuition and creativity. We are acting on this intuition, these new ideas, by using our hands to communicate in a new way, to express ourselves in solid form, in the handmade object. We are, simultaneously, transforming the craft material and, crucially, our mood and ourselves.

> 'I work in a creative industry, but lots of the work I do, day-in and day-out, you could deem not to be creative. If I'm having a stressful week, my pottery is a complete balm. I studied art until I was eighteen and when I had been working for a few years in my twenties, I yearned for some pure creativity, away from work and as an accompaniment to office life.'
> – *Chloe Healy, marketing director, potter*

'I've always wanted to do something creative, but have
usually worked in normal jobs part-time – it is hard
to earn a living as a full-time bookbinder. There was a
period when I had to work full-time in the office and had
little spare time for bookbinding. I feel low if I'm not
being creative. After a day in the studio, it's as though
a weight lifts, it has a therapeutic effect. If I don't have
to worry about earning money, when I'm using my own
creativity to make, it is a real pleasure.'
– Kate Rochester, advertising manager, bookbinding

In *The How of Happiness*, Sonja Lyubomirsky suggests that
happiness has two components: a feeling of contentment or joy
combined with a sense of meaning and purpose in our lives.
Making things makes us happy because pleasure and purpose
meet in meaningful, rewarding creative work with our hands.

Being creative and making things, through the craft and process
that you enjoy, has to bring you joy – there is no point in
continuing to knit, sew, draw or weave if you find it tiresome,
it will only add to your stress stores. So you need to know what
you'd like to make and how you want to make it.
In other words, which craft is right for you? What do you
love doing? We will be looking at this in more detail in
Chapter Six.

Once you've found your craft, it is a small step to start making more things – ergo creativity breeds creativity. And if making makes you happy, you can then create for yourself a greater number of happy moments – happiness breeds happiness. Arzu recalls discovering bookbinding and becoming obsessed with every aspect of putting together a simple hardback book, from waxing the linen thread to making her own sewing frame. This led to learning how to marble paper, how to make *paste papers* and to build more tools to support her new pastime – she drew the line at paper-making but says, 'never say never'.

You also may discover your chosen craft is merely the chapter heading for a host of other crafts.

We looked at Jo Hunter's 65 Million Artists initiative in **Chapter One**. But another piece of research, led by Dr Tamlin S. Conner (University of Ortaga, New Zealand) and others, is just as fascinating. This team of scientists decided to explore the question, 'Does engaging in everyday creative acts make people feel better emotionally?'

The 658 participants who took part in this study kept a diary reporting whether or not they had engaged in creative activities, such as writing, drawing, making music or having an original idea. They were asked to rate their mood and feelings for the duration of the experiment.

With her colleagues, Conner showed that people felt more enthusiasm and generally more positive on the days *after* their creative days, but she also found these results surprising because they were so definitive. Often research data proves inconclusive, but in this study the findings showed definitively that creative activities yielded marked improvements in well-being.

'Doing creative things today predicts improvements in well-being tomorrow. Full stop.'

Results showed that people who were engaged in more creative activities than usual on one day reported increased positive emotion and flourishing on the next, while negative emotions didn't change. However, the reverse effect did not seem to occur: people who experienced higher positive emotions on day one weren't more involved in creative activities on day two, suggesting that everyday creativity leads to more well-being rather than the other way around.

Intriguingly, the study also suggests that personality did not detrimentally affect the positive effects of creativity on well-being, showing that it is likely that some creative activity every day might work for most people. The excellent take away here is that you don't need to feel you have a particularly creative personality or be in any way artistic in order to benefit from a craft pursuit.

'As my confidence in ceramics has grown, it has become an increasingly visible, important part of who I am too. My pottery gives me licence to think and be creative in other parts of my life – I'm not sure how much of that is me giving myself that freedom, or others expecting it of me or bestowing it, but the result is a feeling of confidence, that's the best way I can describe it.'

– *Chloe Healy, marketing director, potter*

ANXIETY, DEPRESSION AND STRESS

'Crochet helped me in my journey to get out of depression and continues to help me maintain mental wellness. It helps me to relax, bringing down levels of anxiety. It gives me a focus for my attention, which helps to reduce the ruminations of the mind that can be so destructive in depression. I have learned how to harness that attention and engage in meditative, mindful crafting specifically to break those patterns of rumination. Crochet gives me something productive to do when it feels hard to do anything, and creating beautiful things for myself and others is a boost to my self-esteem.'

– *Kathryn Vercillo, writer, crocheting*

Mixed anxiety and depression is the most common mental disorder in Britain – in 2014, 19.7% of people in the UK, aged 16 and over, showed symptoms of anxiety and depression – a 1.5% increase from 2013. According to The Mental Health Foundation, 4–10% of people in England will, in their lifetime, suffer from depression.

The factors underlying the rise in cases are complex and varied, but along with genetic predisposition the most common trigger factors are low socio-economic status, gender and work-related stress. The poorer and more disadvantaged – and certain minority and ethnic groups – are disproportionately affected by common mental health problems. In England, women are more likely than men to have a common mental health problem, and are almost twice as likely to be diagnosed with anxiety disorders, while women in full-time employment are nearly twice as likely to have a common mental health problem as full-time employed men.

Workplace stress is increasingly cited as a factor in depressive illness and general anxiety disorders, with 1 in 6.8 people experiencing mental health problems in their jobs (14.7%). Evidence suggests that 12.7% of all sickness absence days in the UK can be attributed to mental health conditions.

Much in the same way that 64 Million Artists believes in an empowered and creatively engaged workforce, we are convinced companies and organisations would do well to provide opportunities for arts for their employees, and believe that this strategy could only benefit staff retention, productivity and loyalty.

Despite the demands on our time and attention from work and family, reuniting the creative self with the self who stresses and frets and occasionally blows things out of proportion is, for us, one way of keeping our lives in balance and can give us the strength of mind to occasionally stand outside a problem and take a more objective view of the situation.

Since 2007, Arts and Minds, a leading arts and mental health charity, has been running weekly art workshops in the community for people experiencing depression, stress or anxiety in Cambridgeshire. Its Arts on Referral project is one of a number of similar NHS primary care initiatives that provide patients with 'prescriptions' for a wide range of craft sessions, including printmaking and sculpture. Crucial to the success of the Arts and Minds workshops is that attendees work alongside fellow makers, skilled teachers and artists in a relaxed, non-clinical setting. The sessions provide support and craft experience, but equally important is the social element of relaxed companionship and connection. This is especially valuable in helping recovery in people who are vulnerable and often socially excluded. The impact has been exceptional with patients, showing a 71% decrease in feelings of anxiety and a 73% falling in depression; 76% of participants said their well-being increased and 69% felt more socially included.

'The particular value of a craft as a "midlife hobby" is of great interest to me. There is a whole process aspect to this: developing a technical skill which involves intense concentration and manual dexterity is very good for the head.'
— *Jim Boddington, GP, potter*

Even in people of an advanced age, brains are flexible and can adapt to their environment — an old dog *can* learn new tricks. This is called neuroplasticity. We can flex our brains by learning new skills and seeking out new experiences – so, we ask, why not learn a new craft?

Studies have found that complex activities such as Sudoku, crossword puzzles or learning a language can help protect against ageing effects on our brain. Scientists are now beginning to study the impact of other hobbies. Results suggest that crafting could reduce the risk of developing mild cognitive impairment by 30–50%.

Although loneliness and social exclusion can afflict anyone at any point in their life, loss of loved ones and ensuing isolation is one of the most significant factors affecting people's health in old age. The Campaign to End Loneliness cites that over 51% of people aged seventy-five and over live alone, according to the Office for National Statistics (2010). Not only that, Age UK found, in 2014, that two-fifths of all older people say that television is their main company. This is another way that craft can play a vital role in improving well-being. Joining a community of fellow makers in a knitting circle, local craft group or through an Arts on Referral initiative like Arts and Minds above provides opportunities to make new friends and connections and becomes an incentive to get out and about.

According to Daisy Fancourt, a growing number of studies demonstrate that taking part in community cultural and arts activities can make a positive impact on early mortality rates, whatever one's socio-economic status and medical history.

As well as an incentive to learn a new skill, joining a local crafting class also aids social identity. We become part of a cohesive community and in turn we benefit from belonging and enjoying the feedback on our work, the sense of team spirit and morale-boosting support.

'Sometimes, in my deepest depressions, I could barely leave my bed, or make it to the fridge to force myself to eat, never mind set foot outside the house. I think we all have times when we just want to hide away, burrow down and stay safe. But when you are deeply, chronically depressed, the endless chatter in your head makes even these seemingly safe spaces a scary option. When I was really ill, I became addicted to quite a few things, things that somehow helped block the pain in my brain, some more benign than others. I'd obsessively work out crossword and code word puzzles, having crawled to the newsagent to buy every newspaper I could lay my hands on. Then I asked a friend who worked at the *Guardian* to send me every volume of the *Quick Crossword Puzzles* she had on her office shelves. Another addiction, weirdly, was *Deal or No Deal*! But I always had my knitting. And that is the thing that I still have on the go all the time – I have one project which has become a kind of talisman because I can't bear to finish it, that's my depression scarf. Thankfully, I haven't had a bad episode of depression for several years. I've got better, moved on and am pursuing many craft projects now, not just knitting, although that remains a constant backdrop to my crafting life. I love

knitting little jumpers for friends' new babies. I knit
bobble hats and scarves and jumpers for my daughter
and sisters and nieces for presents. And just recently I've
been mastering socks. The unfinished "depression scarf"
is still in my knitting bag. It's about four feet long, in a
slightly drab brown, but very soft, wool. I haven't finished
it because maybe I worry that I might need to return to it
if the black cloud descends – or maybe I should just cast
it off, donate it to charity, or give it to someone who will
appreciate its warm, soft, comforting cosiness. And start
another – this time in orange for joy, or for madness!
And celebrate my mental health and surviving to
knit another day.'
— *Rosemary Davidson, editor, crafter*

'At the height of great stress or anxiety it can be difficult
to concentrate on craft. But as issues and problems begin
to resolve, there is hopefully a little more mental space to
consider setting time aside to let the mind wander down
a different path. We have found the benefits to be huge. I
remember the months after my daughter was born. Life,
while often filled with moments of wonder, felt, at times,
like a struggle. Mundane yet essential tasks seemed to
take forever to complete and drain me of any energy I
may have had in reserve that day. It would be absurd to
suggest that one could find the peace of mind (even if
one did have the time or inclination) to sit and knit or
weave with a crying baby, the house in havoc, and a mind

crazed from lack of sleep. But there were moments during those early months when instead of sensibly taking a nap while the baby slept, I would head to my desk, pull out the sheaves of paper, assemble my tools and for an hour, begin to bind a book. Some sessions involved only the gathering and ordering of my tools, but the results of these small interjections into what otherwise often felt the relentless routine of my days were notable. Even if I'd only been at my desk for twenty minutes, I always came away feeling better. The simple pleasure to be gained from measuring sheets of paper, selecting different decorative samples to pair with others, deciding on the structure I would put together, whether a sketchbook, a journal or a photo album, was a great salve to me. Bookbinding was my "thing". I could still do my thing, I wasn't only a person who felt at times like she was failing at this most fundamental of biological imperatives. I was having a hard time, but as long as I could still connect to the me that made books before my baby, I could visualise a point in the future when I wasn't so battered by lack of sleep, and I could return, more fully, to the crafts I enjoyed.'

— *Arzu Tahsin, editor, crafter*

CHAPTER FOUR

Go with the Flow

(How 'craftfulness' is a state of mind)

- -

'Knitting has provided a therapeutic repetitive task
which has helped to calm me and has given me an almost
mindfulness experience. When anxious, it has helped to
slow things down for me.'
– *Helen, blogger, knitting*

Here, Helen is describing the meditative, almost out-of-body
effect of being fully absorbed in a purposeful task, also known
as a state of *flow*.

We can do very little about the families we are born into, or
the time of our birth, or our genetic makeup, yet we all enjoy
moments when we feel totally in control of our lives and the
decisions we make. These wonderful moments, or *optimal
experiences*, tend to occur when we are challenged and engaged –
whether taking part in a sport or a chess game or performing
well in a job interview. We are so absorbed in the activity that
everything outside ceases to exist – as though we are mesmerised.

Interested primarily in the question, *when do people feel most happy?* Hungarian psychologist Dr Mihaly Csikszentmihalyi believes that if we can answer this fundamental conundrum then maybe we can actively order our lives to contain more happiness. He found that happiness does not really depend on outside events, but rather on how we interpret them.

It is from these *optimal experiences* that Csikszentmihalyi developed the term *flow*. Like happiness, however, flow is elusive. And like happiness, it can't simply be acquired. Flow doesn't depend on events or life experiences such as good fortune, money or success happening *to us*, rather it is how *we perceive our experiences*. If we can direct this perception it follows that we can, to some extent, take control of the actual quality of our lives – and this, according to Csikszentmihalyi and other positive psychologists, will bring us as close to happiness as any of us can hope to be.

And while flow is not guaranteed in every activity, the good news for all who are keen to increase their overall happiness quota is that the state of flow is achievable for everyone. The opportunities to experience flow can be cultivated, whether it's by taking up running, learning an instrument or acquiring a new craft skill, for example.

'I generally think I am calmer when I am making. There is a singularity and focus to the task that is sometimes evasive in modern working life. It can help to slow my brain down if I am feeling frazzled, much like sinking into a good book or cooking a meal from scratch. I feel that it engages a different part of my brain and it reminds my hands that they can do more than type and swipe.'
— Emma Smith, publisher, stained-glass designer

In 1963, as part of his doctoral research at the University of Chicago, Csikszentmihalyi studied a group of young artists. He observed their commitment to, and all-consuming absorption and satisfaction in, their work. However, once completed, he noted that the individual artist seemed to lose interest in it. The artwork that had captured their attention for the duration of the actual painting was often stacked in the corner, along with all the other canvasses, to all appearances forgotten.

He was curious to understand why these artists' absorption in the actual process of the work was so driven, given that very few of the extrinsic incentives that motivate hard work were present: they were not spurred on by possessing the finished canvas or by the prospect of financial reward or fame. Csikszentmihalyi concluded that what motivated them was *making* the painting. The process itself was what they prized.

Other examples of Csikszentmihalyi's early research sampled the experiences of thousands of people from around the world and from different walks of life. Whatever the activity, for those who described what he came to term his world-famous concept, *the state of flow,* the characteristics of the experience were the same: a focused state of concentration and a feeling of satisfaction while engaged in the pursuit. This state of flow wasn't exclusive to artists; those engaged in sports, musicians, builders, computer programmers and teachers reported the same level of immersion.

Csikszentmihalyi remarked that people who lost themselves in their work shared similar states of absorption to children at play: in full flow, wholly engaged with the task at hand, the outside world ceases to exist.

> 'Knitters often talk about going into the "zone" when they knit. It can be total chaos around you but you carry on regardless, totally and happily oblivious to everyone and everything. It's like taking one big glorious and healthy happy pill.'
> — *Jacqui Fink, extreme knitter, fibre artist*

CHILDREN AND FLOW

We have all watched children playing and probably marvelled at the apparent fact that they can become so engrossed in a game or activity that the world outside might as well be on another planet. Watching the very young create personalities for their toys and invent entire landscapes in which free-form narratives unfurl is intriguing. Their state of flow is entirely instinctive. The child is fully engrossed in the game, focus on the next instalment does not waver, the outside world or the voices of parents calling them to tea do not register.

As children we flow naturally. And as we grow we develop constantly by evolving new skills to meet new challenges. At school, the opportunities for unstructured, imaginative play are a little more limited and as we climb the academic ladder, they are fewer still. By adulthood, most of us have forgotten that blissful feeling of utterly losing ourselves in an activity.

Flow is most likely to be experienced when we are involved in a pursuit in which we are fully enthralled. The ideal, of course, is to find this state of total captivation in our day jobs, or even in housework, and while this remains a possibility in both instances, it may not be realistic (or in the latter, desirable) for everyone.

'It's not a panacea. Inevitably the truth is – it's never as simple as that. The emotions of a making practice mirror real life. So there is enjoyment, ecstasy, etc., there's also boredom, irritation, fury, ennui. Always the inner dialogue goes on: to worry less about the product, the outcome – engage again with the process, with the ideas, with the problem solving. There's a kind of internal Zen monk at work, trying to dial down the childlike "aren't I clever" position. When it all works though, it's that same

sense of a part of one's brain, and whole being, opening up, turned on to our dream states. The space you can get into probably is some kind of place out of time, an ideal platonic space defined by the language of form and elements that you're playing and working with.'
– Will Brook, GP, woodworker

'When I'm drawing I feel calm, clear, peaceful, happy. Occasionally frustrated and lost, but working through that feeling is really just a metaphor for my life as an adult.'
– Danny Gregory, The Creative License

As a technique for stilling the mind, for absorbing one's attention, for distraction from our daily stresses and concerns, this state of flow is a key element in any well-being practice.

Csikszentmihalyi underlines that by learning how to control our experiences and introduce flow into our activities, we can overcome the obstacles to fulfilment and enjoy a richer, more meaningful life.

This may seem like a tall order, but whether it's a solitary walk in the woods or a daily meditation, the goal is to abandon ourselves entirely to it, to separate ourselves from our internal struggles and the concerns of the day for a short while and shift our focus to a space where our thoughts aren't all-consuming.

The concept of flow is central to 'craftfulness'. The ability to lose oneself in the task at hand is one of the great components of making, the benefits of which make an impact on your life, long after you have put away your tools.

> 'I have to give my work enough dedicated time to go into a zone. I have a rough plan of what I want to make, but for it to go beyond something which is just a project you have to give it time – it becomes its own thing. It has a life of its own – and I am not conscious of process when I'm in that zone, the ideas come from places I am unaware of, *then it gets really exciting.*'
> – *Kate Young, occupational therapist, drawing, painting*

Once we have enjoyed the flow state during a regular activity or hobby, it is relatively easy to tap back into it. It is also a deeply compelling state to be in. If you meditate regularly or are already practising some form of craft using your hands or perhaps are a keen runner, you will know the flow state well, and already be aware of the feeling and its many benefits.

But how does it work exactly? Neuroscience has shown that the flow state induces the release of a chemical called dopamine, responsible for transmitting signals between the nerve cells of the brain. Dopamine is associated with motivation and reward as well as regulating mood, behaviour, sleep and concentration. Too little of this powerful chemical can leave you feeling unfocused and de-motivated. Studies have shown that natural flow states lead to greater dopamine release.

As is pertinent to any well-being practice, there is a growing body of scientific evidence indicating that those of us who regularly experience the flow state develop positive traits such as increased concentration, self-esteem and performance. These traits encourage meaning in our lives and promote self-confidence; we might then add new pursuits and increase our repertoire of exciting extra-curricular activities.

The experience of flow not only boosts well-being, but also acts as a magnet for learning, for developing new skills and challenges.

HOW DO WE KNOW
IF WE ARE EXPERIENCING FLOW?

'While making, I have a feeling that I have become fully myself, using mediums that provide a sensory experience that suits me. The very tactile experience of cutting, manipulating different printing tools and running my fingers through the paper or the cloth, results in the ability to understand better who I am. I often dispose of the image that I have just drawn, and I rarely look back at my prints or embroideries. As an art therapist, I am aware that there is a life in a finished picture, but I feel that, in my case, the process of making images is more important than the resulting picture. I enjoy the making and I feel a lot of satisfaction in using all kinds of printmaking techniques that require attention and patience. In all my artwork, I tend to spend hours working on details, going through the same line or the same stitch, in a repetitive manner. This gives me a real sense of relaxation and calm. I love the excitement around the end of the printing process. I am very keen to learn new stitches and improve my standard of craftsmanship but the artwork I produce is essentially an expression of my feelings at the time and I consider that this is most important.'

– Anne-Catherine le Deunff, art therapist,
printmaker

While Csikszentmihalyi's thesis concluded that flow is a universal experience with many different components, he defined a number of key characteristics common to all respondents. It is worth looking at some of these in a little depth, as they reveal simple steps to finding the right mindful activity for you. A large part of this comes down to your own taste and preference, but whichever materials you prefer to work with, be it wool and thread or paper and simple maths, within each discipline there is a world of opportunity for evolving your skillset and using it to make work which exercises your creative muscles.

- *The task must have a goal and a clear set of rules, necessary for direction and structure*: In this case, it's craft rather than task. With crafts, the goals are not always as clear as, for example, those of chess or learning to play a musical instrument. It is useful, however, to establish a strong personal sense of what your finished piece should look like, while following the basic steps to achieve the idea. This will keep you motivated. To get started, rules are important, but without bending rules there would be no innovation or creativity. Once we have achieved a certain level of proficiency, our imagination can experiment beyond the confines of the rules.

- *The task at hand must have clear and immediate feedback which allows us to adjust our work and maintain the flow state*: This point refers to understanding where you are going wrong and getting back on track. This is important when learning a new skill, but later, when your confidence has grown, you may begin to feel that the tangents we take lead to more interesting work and set alight new ideas to drive creativity. The more we are able to shift between our ambition and our ability to experiment, the greater our capacity for achieving flow.

- *It should be a challenging activity that requires skill*: The goals are attainable, yet at the same time you are challenged by the process, giving you the opportunity to develop your skillset. Here is where we advise you to break out of your comfort zone. The extra concentration required to follow a different set of rules focuses the mind beautifully. This balancing act between challenge and skill is what keeps us so engaged when we are making.

- *We must be able to concentrate on what we are doing*: To lose yourself in an activity is the way to achieve flow. If we are focused on the task at hand, the many distractions of our surroundings, the circling thoughts are, for a short while, silenced. In the early stages of acquiring new skills, it is worth allowing yourself the space and time to concentrate without disruption. Later, when you are in complete mastery of a craft you might find that you can find yourself in a flow state, no matter where you are – as when Rosemary is knitting and completely oblivious to her children's conversation around her or their attempts to get an answer to a question.

'I loved having to concentrate when I was a therapist, listening to clients who often brought distressing problems. Working with fabric was a way to relax, be creative, and experience the real joy of colour, texture, patterns, etc. I love working with graph paper and felt-tipped pens – time passes very rapidly, and it is the perfect antidote to counselling – at least it was for me. The mind is free to wander, but the satisfaction

of producing something which is tactile, practical and
attractive gives immense pleasure.'
— *Jean Holloway, retired psychotherapist, needlework*

- *There should be a merging of action and awareness*: This requires
  a level of involvement with your work that feels almost
  automatic. *Spontaneity* is the key word here, action follows
  action, effortlessly. Now, you can lose all sense of time and
  the outside world and although your crafting skills might
  appear effortless to others, it is far from being so. You are in
  the rhythm of making and the concerns of the day are, for a
  short while, muted.

There's a lot to absorb here, but if you can remember these
characteristics when starting a craft, you are well on your way to
making the most of your new pastime.

'Whilst drawing a landscape, for example, where you are
using your skills in a precise way, more like a technical
drawing – I find that very therapeutic, it takes me out
of my head. It doesn't require an emotional engagement,
just observation. To be really observant you can't be
thinking about your own feelings. It is an almost clinical,
mathematical process, adjusting tone, depth, detail.
It can be very relaxing.'
— *Kate Young, occupational therapist, drawing,*
painting

PART II

CHAPTER FIVE

Getting Over Negativity
(Or when 'no' becomes 'maybe' and 'maybe' becomes 'yes!')

Understanding what might be holding you back is the first step in any new endeavour. As we have touched on earlier in this book, one of the barriers to starting any new activity – a career change, a degree, a new business, craft or hobby – is the fear of failure, and worse, failing in front of others. If you have always dreamed of throwing a pot or making a Fair Isle jumper, but have held back because of self-doubt or a mistaken belief that you don't have the talent, join the club. But the difference between failure and succeeding is having a go. And those who try are 100% more likely to succeed than those who never pick up their needles, book a pottery class, or apply for a new job.

'Remembering that I'll be dead soon is the most important tool I've ever encountered to help me make the big choices in life. Because almost everything – all external expectations, all pride, all fear of embarrassment or failure – these things just fall away in the face of death, leaving only what is truly important.'

– Steve Jobs, entrepreneur, co-founder of Apple, inventor

These words from Steve Jobs are often quoted in motivational speeches and have lost none of their power in the repetition. While acknowledging we are focusing on a craft practice in the pursuit of well-being, rather than a radical life change, the point remains that a positive, open, can-do mindset is more likely to lead to new opportunities, as well as equip us with the tools to face challenges with confidence and courage. When we mute the insidious voice telling us, 'you can't do that, you're not talented enough', the obstacles in our way tend to become significantly more manageable. Fear of failure is no impediment to trying.

NEGATIVE EMOTIONS ARE PART AND PARCEL OF BEING HUMAN. BUT IT'S NOT ALL BAD.

Paradoxically, even negativity has its uses. It has been shown that negative experiences – fears, feelings or difficult events – have a greater impact on our psychological state than positive ones. This isn't particularly surprising. When we have enough food to eat, and a roof over our heads, we don't live in a state of constant gratitude. As long as we don't have to *worry* about going hungry or being cold, we can simply adjust to our circumstances – even take them completely for granted. However, the memory of traumatic events or nagging fears and feelings of hurt, humiliation, resentment, jealousy can continue to colonise our thoughts long after.

The reason for this disparity is that our biological and psychological response to negative events is hardwired: fear of pain or danger helps to keep us out of harm's way; bad news signals potential for disaster. While we are far less likely to face the hazards of our evolutionary ancestors, the body and the brain's magnetic attraction to adverse stimuli is innate.

In other words, a little bit of psychological negativity is healthy and natural. But it should work *for us*, not against us. We want to be able to limit the impact of negative thoughts on our ability to move on and get on with our lives; to make good choices, dream a little and take chances.

Managing anxiety is one of the key benefits of a daily craft or well-being practice. Our craft practices have, unquestionably, helped us to manage stress and limit persistent, intrusive and unhelpful thoughts. It is not merely distraction, but rather an active engagement with a task that is completely absorbing and creatively stimulating which aids in resetting one's perspective on how we deal with everyday crises.

Let's look at how we can quieten those voices of insecurity.

Fear can kill success. That might sound like another clichéd statement, but it is worth deconstructing. What is at the root of our fear? Why might we turn away from opportunity? If we avoid taking up a new hobby, learning a new craft, engaging in exercise, then we have already decided the outcome. It might have been a failure, but we didn't even give ourselves the chance to succeed.

One interesting theory about the fear of failure is that what we really fear is not getting it right the first time. In this book, we are not advocating that the craft practice you engage in or are already pursuing has perfection as its goal. We are trying out new skills: we hope you find one or two activities that resonate with you and go on to bring you pleasure. Admittedly, some crafts are trickier than others, but you may also find that the more fiddly aspects are themselves part of the appeal.

The first time you make a piece of work you are truly happy with, you are also looking at all the pieces you deemed failures. You persisted by correcting previous errors, improving and streamlining the process and you probably did all of this in a state of flow. If you enjoy your practice, the finished item is a display of contentment, commitment and perseverance.

Most of us have some fears about the future, but the greater our fear the more likely we are to procrastinate. Fear is an emotion that we can choose to engage with to a greater or lesser degree.

If you're reading this book, then you are ready to engage with a new chapter in your life, one that includes mindful practice. You may begin clumsily, fail to observe the instructions correctly, produce a piece of work you want to dispose of quickly (and maybe secretly!), but you have not failed: you have taken the first step on the road towards finding a mindful preoccupation.

Challenging certain negative assumptions we have held on to for as long as we've had memories is a profoundly empowering exercise. We may realise that doing one thing differently, whether in our work or our relationships, can make a huge impact on self-confidence and thus the faith that we have some control over our lives.

When she started bookbinding, Arzu saw only the flaws in her first notebooks – the covers that were askew, the uneven pages, the unsightly glue stains on the spines ... But after a moment, her focus would shift and she saw not only the time it took to make the book but the mental application and patience that went into measuring, cutting, folding: the pleasure in making. Of course, we might set out to craft the perfect book, but the object in her hands, while not perfect by any means, reflects an investment of time and pleasure.

DEALING WITH SELF-DOUBT

'Forget talent. It's a meaningless concern. Maybe you
have it, maybe you don't, whatever. Don't let this issue
become an excuse for not trying what you dream of doing.
What matters is valuing yourself and expanding
what you can do.'
— *Danny Gregory*, *The Creative License*

If you have ever attempted a creative project or craft and felt
you hadn't mastered it as you had hoped (perhaps the project
demanded greater manual dexterity, or the finished item wasn't
nearly as beautiful as your instructions promised), you may
believe that craft is not for you. You might want to achieve a
certain standard in your drawing, for example, and envy friends
who effortlessly translate what they see in front of them onto the
page with a few easy flourishes of their pen. They are *naturally
gifted*, you assume, and by comparison you see your own efforts
as clumsy, childish, embarrassing.

But we have yet to meet a single artist who believes that
drawing is a talent you are born with. Quite the opposite: they
all enthusiastically encourage continued effort. Keep going, they
say, the more you draw, the better you will become and the more
you will enjoy it.

We learn by trial and error. It is a cliché, but mistakes are an
opportunity to improve.

At times, of course, we all experience frustration when our projects wander up the path of no return, but we don't very often just give up. Rosemary has recently had issues with some pumpkins, for example. It started with a neighbour's children helping to weed and dig in her front garden. Within days their friends took part, as did their friends' friends, and soon the number of little helpers started to expand quite fast. Rosemary then had the bright idea of buying seeds, pots and compost to grow some pumpkins, of the Giant American variety, with the children. A mistake in an order of fresh horse manure meant that an articulated lorry delivered three pallets of best organic matter to her front door, taking up three parking spaces. And the pumpkin plants grew and grew and grew, taking over the front garden, the walls, spilling over on to the pavement. But not a single fruit grew to maturity.

The excess manure and the disappointing lack of monster pumpkins didn't really matter though. What had been so joyful was the afternoons spent out there with a bunch of curious and wide-eyed local Jewish children all mucking in and delighting in the process of planting, tending and watering during those unusually blistering summer days of 2017. Undaunted, they took stock, composted the barren pumpkin vines, and then started again with some low-maintenance vegetable seeds. And have been chomping the harvest of rainbow chard all winter. It's even survived the cold snap and Siberian snow. Sometimes you have to take a break or turn to a new idea. Rosemary and her team of junior gardeners are planning to sow some smaller pumpkins, tomatoes, basil, courgettes and some spinach in late spring, early summer.

Occasionally, we get stuck on a project because it involves a tricky step, stitch or techique that we are unfamiliar with and we need to turn to a book or YouTube for instructions. If we get really stuck, we might decide to ask for advice from others or take formal lessons to focus on improving or learning the skills which will make a difference to the work.

The destination is important, but the journey even more so, and we find that the finished piece takes care of itself once we are on the road.

'My mum taught me how to knit as a child, but I never committed to learning the language of knitting so my skills remained very basic. When I think about it, I don't think I ever finished a single project. Then, as it is now, my focus was on the therapeutic quality of the exercise, not the functionality. Similarly, it was always the journey that I found rewarding, not the outcome.'
– *Jacqui Fink, extreme knitter, fibre artist*

WABI-SABI – LEARNING TO LOVE IMPERFECTION

'I used to be a very impatient person, working in a fast-paced industry in a state of constant urgency. Everything had to be controlled and precise. Ceramics has taught me to let go. I have become a more patient person, more careful and considered in my responses. My pots aren't perfect. I've learned to enjoy the freedom in creativity.

Pottery involves a lot of failure, but you have to learn to take it on the chin and the more you make, the more you learn and learn to let go of the mistakes. A lot of your work is left to chance, once your work is in the kiln, it's also in the lap of the gods. I have learned to embrace the happy accidents.'

— Ranjit Dhaliwal, picture researcher, potter

As we've been at pains to point out, neither of us can lay any claim to being an expert crafter. We are self-taught and, while we're conscientious makers, often the things we produce are far from perfect.

Of course, our intention to craft pleasing objects we can feel proud of is paramount — that's part of the joy of learning new skills or evolving dormant ones and just generally challenging ourselves. It wouldn't be nearly as satisfying to have low expectations or to do the bare minimum; that would very quickly guarantee a loss of interest as well as wasting time and resources. But part of our approach to making things is accepting the inevitability of, and being comfortable with, imperfection. Perhaps for us that's the only way to embark on any endeavour.

Making something as well as we can and being ambitious, however, is satisfying. The care, concentration and focus and the time spent purposefully in the process is rewarding on so many levels. But part and parcel of our 'craftfulness' ethos, our *tao of making*, is being prepared for mistakes when they happen, to take a deep breath when all is not going to plan and to accept that veering off the path occasionally may lead to interesting avenues of creative diversion. And, crucially, to not give up or feel dispirited by blotches, blobs of glue and dropped stitches; but instead, to live with some irregularity and consider how these imperfect pieces reflect something of ourselves in their asymmetry. We're not machines, after all.

Acceptance of imperfection and learning to appreciate beauty in the unevenness and sometimes very simple, rustic feel of our everyday craftworks is key to our *wabi-sabi* approach to craft and to making.

Wabi-sabi is a Japanese concept that originated in the customs and rituals of the Zen Tea Ceremony and the Tea Masters. Part aesthetic and part philosophy of life, *wabi-sabi* has an elusive definition and no exact equivalent translation in English. The best introduction to the idea is in Leonard Koren's *Wabi-Sabi for Artists, Designers, Poets & Philosphers*, in which he writes; 'Wabi-sabi in its fullest expression can be a way of life. At the very least, it is a particular type of beauty ... of things imperfect, impermanent and incomplete. It is a beauty of things humble. It is a beauty of things unconventional.'

Sabi, Koren explains, is an ancient word dating to eighth-century Japan, derived from Chinese poetry, when its meaning was 'to be desolate'; it then evolved to mean 'taking pleasure in that which is old, faded and lonely' and to describe the beauty of things that are worn, incomplete, imperfect and mismatched. *Wabi*, like *sabi*, is also an ancient word that originally meant 'to apologise deeply, humbly' and only later assumed the 'poetically positive connotations' of feeling lonesome and forlorn. The meanings of the words evolved to such a degree that they are today more or less interchangeable: *wabi* frequently meaning *sabi*, and vice versa.

Associated with Zen Buddhism, there are also spiritual and metaphysical aspects to *wabi-sabi*. And Koren suggests the term could even be called 'the Zen of things', as it exemplifies so much of Zen's core spiritual–philosophical tenets.

Wabi-sabi is being comfortable with the passing of time and the impermanence of things and people and as Koren so beautifully puts it: 'All comes to nothing in the end. Everything wears down. The planets and the stars, even intangibles like reputation, family heritage, historical memory, scientific theorems, mathematical proofs, great art and literature – all eventually fade into oblivion and nonexistence.' In its acceptance of the inevitable, Koren says, *wabi-sabi* 'forces us to contemplate our own impermanence, our mortality, stirs a bittersweet comfort since we know all existence shares the same fate.'

'Even the failures that come off the wheel are not a waste of time or materials. With clay, up until the moment you decide to fire your piece, you can reclaim and reuse it. Growing up, God forbid you should attempt something that might not work. If you failed it would be a disaster, everything had to be a success. Clay reconstitutes and provides a learning experience, there isn't waste. It doesn't have to be permanent until you decide it has to be permanent, you don't have to use lots of resources to then see it as a failure.'

– Clare Spindler, potter

The *wabi-sabi* aesthetic or way of life chimes with our craft ethos and the spirit of 'craftfulness' in several important ways. Primarily, in that it is about finding beauty and value in the imperfect and the very ordinary, *wabi-sabi* redefines beauty as a matter of perception: unassuming, modest, coarse objects, ugly things, if you like, become beautiful on deeper contemplation. Beauty, like happiness, and like creativity, is a state of mind – this is an incredibly comforting concept and guiding principle, when you think about it.

So, too, is the idea that irregular or old, used and worn items that are rusty, eroded, patched, glued or repaired are all the more beautiful and precious *because* of their imperfections. The glitches, tears, loose threads, holes, cracks, smears or dents on an object, along with marks of age and use, carry a memory of the hands of the people who made them; of those that have used, reused and repaired them; and of time's ineluctable march.

'I make functional pottery out of clay. I like the idea of it being used, the sense that someone will like the piece enough to take it home. It might be just another cereal bowl to you, but it was made by me. I like the thought of the constant presence of these handmade objects. The idea of making something beautiful and functional. The use of these objects is key, and the cracks and chips they accumulate along the way tells their story in the household.'

— *Clare Spindler, potter*

'Craftfulness' is not just about making new things, new objects from scratch. Careful and mindful consumption, the spirit of 'make do and mend', recycling and finding use and beauty in things that others might reject, discard, overlook are important principles, too.

Mending, darning, repairing and recycling are absolutely key to our way of thinking. As mass-market production has driven down the cost and value of everyday items, we have become used to discarding things that are no longer quite perfect and simply buying more new disposable things. We rarely take the time to fix anything anymore – it's so easy to buy new with just one click. Learning how to darn a jumper or re-sew a seam or a hem might sound painstakingly laborious and irksome, but from experience, and as we will explore later, once mastered there is the reward of feeling intense satisfaction when a cherished wardrobe stalwart has been rescued by your own efforts.

Artist Celia Pym has turned darning into an art form. 'I love seeing damage and holes. Making mending invisible doesn't make sense for me: things happen, stuff changes, holes appear. Let the darning grow into the old bit so that the garment can be seen to change and age.' The same applies for mending any household item – it takes a little bit of time and care, but with some sturdy glue or the wonder product that is Sugru, most things can be given a new lease of life. The loom building and weaving and visible mending projects featured in Part III will show every keen crafter how easy it is to make patches and creative darns for beloved and worn clothes.

Sometimes, old and threadbare garments are simply so damaged as to be beyond repair, or some, annoyingly, get ruined by accidents on the hot cycle in the washing machine, but they, too, can be repurposed; shrunken jumpers can be used in felting or as stuffing for cushions, toys and ragdolls. Threadbare sheets, children's hand-me-downs or old shirts can be cut up and used in quilting and patching – or, as a last resort, used as rags for cleaning.

If a bowl or teacup is cracked or broken, the Japanese have another *wabi-sabi* tradition called *Kintsugi* (also called *Kintsukuroi*), in which the pieces are first glued back together, and ceramic gold paint applied over the fissure to create something unique and useful. And, if it is leaky, then use it to make a little indoor succulent garden, for example (see 'Make a clay pinch pot', p. 158).

Making things more consciously has helped us to appreciate the cost of the beautiful things we see in shops or on Etsy – not just the price of the materials, but the human expenditure of labour, of skill and of time. Rosemary is now less inclined to buy mass-produced items that she doesn't *really need* – in fact, she thinks there's another side-effect to crafting in that it's partially cured her shopaholic tendencies. Maybe it's the upside of the mindful and meditative nature of knitting and pottery, but these days she has less want or need to boost her mood with small gifts to herself. She is too busy knitting socks, so spends less time idly looking at online shops or becoming fixated by the sales. Instead, she now gets weirdly excited by the prospect of an evening of Swiss darning!

'Crafting for me is a tiny little action against mass consumption and mass production. If you feel like you can make your own things, you can realise your own creativity and power to make, rather than buy. It can also make you appreciate the work that does go into handcrafted things and feel more connected to objects around you.'
— *Emma Smith, publisher, stained-glass designer*

You may believe you are not a creative person; maybe your previous attempts led nowhere and you became discouraged. Some level of effort is required to learn any new skill, and as we have seen in the digger rats' experiment in Chapter Two, this can be hugely rewarding. While in the past, you may not have committed fully to learning the techniques required to reach a standard you are happy with, to be happier with your work, it is important to value the challenge of learning and improving. With craft activities, our heads and hands have to find a way of working together, which for many of us is easier said than done; patience more than skill is essential to achieve incremental progress. Sometimes, adopting the mindset of a child at play can unleash the courage to simply have a go. Picasso's observation is key to understanding how our beliefs about our own abilities and talents should be challenged, 'Every child is an artist. The problem is how to remain an artist once he grows up.'

As we saw in Chapter Four with Csikszentmihalyi's *flow* study, as children, our creativity is encouraged and stimulated, but as we move up through education, there is less time for messy play, making 'stuff' and writing stories; we have fewer opportunities for expressing ourselves through arts and crafts. The freedom to indulge our imaginations is often curtailed by a parent's academic expectations, the curriculum, pressures of exams, making a life plan or choosing a profession, but none of this should exclude the value of play.

Ken Robinson's 2006 Ted Talk, 'Do schools kill creativity?' has been viewed online over 40 million times and seen by an estimated 350 million people in 160 countries, making it the most viewed Ted Talk of all time. His contention is that creativity is as important in education as literacy. As children, we aren't scared to have a go at things, we take chances and don't worry too much about being wrong. By the time we're adults, however, we have lost that capacity and Robinson asks, how will we come up with anything original if we're not prepared to be wrong? He says that schools are partly responsible for steering children away from subjects they enjoy which are unlikely to lead to a fruitful career; he believes that many brilliantly creative aspirations are stifled because they are undervalued in our education system. This is not to blame parents or teachers, but rather to look at the system which puts so much emphasis on academic achievement.

'The message from my childhood was that we kids should be good at maths and science. My father was an engineer and my life was very much focused on the objective success which came from exams and tests. I learned to follow careful sets of instructions which in turn led to specific goals. Pottery has been a release from the expectation that everything has to be planned and thought through and even more the expectation that I have to be good at those things.'
— *Clare Spindler, potter*

GIVE YOURSELF PERMISSION

Danny Gregory, author of *The Creative License: Giving Yourself Permission to Be the Artist You Truly Are,* believes that you can express yourself creatively if you give yourself permission and take some risks. Gregory's views on creativity are stimulating. He argues that we all have a powerful creative energy and if we continually suppress it we risk narrowing our worldview, shutting ourselves off to new ideas and people.

Gregory suggests that waiting for the muse to arrive might take a very long time, and that getting into the mood to make comes from action, believing that once you put pen to paper you are most of the way to filling the page.

We can think of a million reasons not to engage with any well-being pursuit, but we also know that lacking faith in your own potential is an unrewarding experience, leaving us feeling low and depleted of energy. It is also habit forming and can spread to every area of our lives if we let it.

Sometimes taking the opposite view can surprise you in the best way. When you are feeling stuck, it can be helpful to consider new ways of resolving familiar or recurring problems. Some of us find positive thinking very easy; the natural inclination is to look for the upside in a bad situation or to use a bad experience as an opportunity. For others, it takes some work. The tools to help form new and better habits are all around us now, but we have to take that first step. And with that step comes momentum, leading to the second and third steps, and before long we are walking with confidence. This might sound clichéd and like a tiresome *positive thinking* slogan, but it is only our own initiative which determines how we approach the obstacles in our lives.

Julia Cameron, in *The Artist's Way: A Course in Discovering and Recovering Your Creative Self,* offers various and inspiring tools to help unlock your creative nature. She suggests there are many reasons why we don't engage with our creative pursuits, such as the fear of what others will say or that creativity is a luxury. However, she believes that when we decide to quieten these voices and do what we love (or grow to love), we unlock potential. Negative beliefs, she asserts, are just that: *beliefs*, not facts.

You may have forgotten the skills you once mastered or feel too clumsy to take up embroidery or woodworking again. But it is important to remember there is no audience and no teacher to grade your work. You may judge your own work harshly, we're only human after all, but that is no impediment to creativity. By deciding what you would like to do, by making the time to do it, you will feel a sense of achievement and experience the gratifying knowledge that you followed your heart and made something yourself.

There is joy in discovering the right craft pursuit for you and using your imagination to create the things you only dreamed about. To finish a craft project, you have to *start* a craft project. You have to pick up the pen, thread the needle and dust off your sewing machine. You must devote some time to a discipline, which will soon feel as natural a part of your life as watching TV!

By giving yourself permission to try, you are halfway to establishing a creative routine. In order to take up any new activity, you just need to believe that no one is holding you back.

BE PREPARED

In his book, *Finding Your Zone,* sports psychiatrist Michael Lardon describes his work with athletes to help them achieve their potential. He suggests some great techniques for athletes to get in the *zone* and achieve a *flow state* in their sport. Lardon's work with athletes also provides valuable insights into how we all can build self-confidence and aim higher.

We have tailored his tips for embarking on a new project or learning a new craft:

Build on mastery experiences: pay close attention to the process and not necessarily the goal. It takes time and a keen focus to improve our skills. Dedication to process, while richly rewarding in itself, leads to projects you are proud to share with others. The more time you put into your practice, the more pride you feel when your project begins to resemble the image in your head, not to mention the pleasure gained from concentration and the *flow state*.

Apply vicarious learning: research your chosen craft project, and use examples and instructions from your reading or internet searches to inspire your own efforts. Join craft forums, ask questions, set up informal craft groups. Expanding your ambition is rewarding, not just for your craft, but also for your confidence and energetic engagement with others.

Find a model that inspires you: This is Colossal (www.thisiscolossal .com) is a wonderful website which inspires us daily with a plethora of intriguing art from around the world. While we might only attempt to incorporate a couple of ideas into our own work, poring over such beautifully crafted pieces has an overall impact on our perception of ourselves as makers. We feel part of the narrative. Visit galleries and museums, follow inspirational Instagram accounts, start a Pinterest board, treat yourself to a couple of new art magazines or inspiring illustrated craft manuals.

Believe in positive reinforcement: starting any new activity, whether learning a new language or taking up a sport or a craft activity, requires a degree of self-belief which only you can initiate. There are many reasons not to add another activity to your life – restrictions on your time, lack of belief in your abilities, the hurdle of starting from scratch – but these are what we call full stop thoughts. They shut down a conversation and negate opportunity.

Which pretty much sums up everything we've looked at so far.

CHAPTER SIX

Making Time & Space
(To stretch your imagination and flex your fingers)

- -

'My drawings are often made in an absent mood, anywhere, at any time of the day or night. The process in printmaking requires more commitment and more energy so I need to think ahead and find some time during the holiday or weekends. I tend to work quickly, directly onto the metal plate, the linoleum, the wood or the canvas, so it can be done at home when I find an hour or two in the week.

'Lately, I have concentrated on my work as an art therapist, encouraging adults and children in my sessions to use the art materials, while feeling frustrated that I have little time to do my own art. I felt that there was something lacking in my life. During my spare time, at home, I started to work on a series of drypoints. I realised that this was helping me keep in touch with my own voice, bringing to light some of the issues which may have otherwise remained inarticulate.'

— *Anne-Catherine le Deunff, art therapist, printmaker*

How we invest what free time we have is important, but, realistically, the decision is not entirely our own to make if we head straight into childcare from work, or we're caring for elderly or sick relatives or studying.

It *feels* as though there are more demands on our time than ever before, even though we were promised the digital revolution would also revolutionise our working week. If, in reality, we are not actually busier, why do we feel as though we are? As we all know now, there are in fact constant demands on our attention. How many of us watch TV with iPhone in hand, while having supper? We might be checking social media, or the cast list of actors in the film we're watching; it's a particular type of multitasking where the actual task is never actually completed. This is one way we end up feeling overwhelmed by the pressures on our time. When we leave work, we don't leave our inbox at the office, it's usually in our pockets, and then it's in the kitchen, while we prepare meals, and often beside our dinner plates, when we finally sit down to eat.

Part of the problem with time management has to do with perception. In *Scarcity: Why Having Too Little Means So Much*, economist Sendhil Mullainathan and behaviourial scientist Eldar Shafir conducted research which led them to conclude that if we believe we have very little of something, be it time, money or food, then a mindset of *scarcity* sets in. The perception of not having quite *enough* focuses the mind on the lack of it and, in turn, creates tunnel vision, where we then shut ourselves off to creative solutions and good decisions.

There is room in all our lives for personal choice, and how we spend our (albeit limited) free time is one of the most important in terms of taking care of our mental health and well-being.

Let's look at how we can make this happen. Take the fact that much of our free time is spent in the digital realm.

Michael Winnick, founder and CEO of dscout, an online research tool, and his team conducted a study which revealed we touch our phones on average around 2,617 times a day. And it doesn't take a genius to deduce that our ability to focus on a single task for an extended period can be inhibited by the proximity of our digital media. Whether it's engaging in social media or watching boxed sets, this is obviously one area where we might be able to siphon off some time for other activities. Watching television might stop the mind from unravelling due to stress, but a constructive practice will give us, in the long run, the power to shape a better quality of life. And, as we have seen, hobbies or skills that require a level of engagement conducive to *flow* are much better placed to accommodate the part of our lives devoted to well-being.

'I am quite organised. I think a lot about what I'm going to draw or paint before I do it. I draw very regularly, I can do it anywhere, it's a habit. My collages take a little planning, they can become a project management exercise, but I always have one on the go, almost like knitting.'
– *Kate Young, occupational therapist, drawing, painting*

There are benefits to be had from imposing a short daily curfew on our devices. For the *flow* state to be engaged, we must dedicate all our attention to the task at hand.

> 'When I was working full-time it was quite hard to find time to sew but I would always try to put aside a couple of hours especially at the weekend to make something. Knitting is a little easier as it is more transportable. It was always important to do something for myself, as it helped me to relax and to be in my own space both in a physical and emotional sense. Since being retired I have the opportunity to do a lot more and now have a dedicated sewing room where I can do what I want. It's great! Now I do a lot more quilting, dressmaking and knitting and of course weaving.'
> *– Pauline Smith, retired teacher, quilter*

By making time for a well-being practice we distance ourselves from the concerns of our everyday lives. Whether that time takes place after the children are in bed, or when we switch our phones to silent, it is a short period of respite for oneself. This space – physical and mental – is where ideas can flourish and ignite inspiration. Those who practise daily meditation know well how this quiet time can be re-energising, enabling a reconnection with the outside world that doesn't feel quite so combative.

> 'I tend to my creative practice every day of the week in some capacity. But it isn't a juggle. It's just a way of life

now. It is as fundamental to me as breathing. There are times when the demands of my business take me away from the physical making. Interestingly, I have found that these separations cause me to lose my centre. The good news is I can now recognize the signs and all it takes is for me to pick up my knitting needles and just commune for a while with some beautiful wool.'

– Jacqui Fink, extreme knitter, fibre artist

ROUTINE

We all live in the real world and developing a craft habit might seem easier said than done, for two main reasons. Who has the time to devote to picking up an old craft hobby or learning a new skill, you might ask?

Firstly, most of us tend to live within the constraints of our everyday routine – a zone of comfort for negotiating the demands of our lives. Routine is important, of that there is little doubt: without routine imagine the mind-blowing number of tiny decisions we would have to make every single day.

But plodding from one dutiful task to the next can begin to feel exhausting, and worse, boring: our autopilot function seems to be on – *all the time*. Too much routine puts up a boundary around our lives; we live within the constraints of the rules we have imposed.

Part of what holds some of us back as creators is a reluctance to start something that might take us out of our comfort zone, a project that disrupts the routine on which we so heavily rely to negotiate the demands on our time and attention. Working a nine-to-five job or studying part-time or caring for children or aging parents might feel like insurmountable obstacles requiring a major overhaul rather than a small re-jig of our lives. But even within these constraints there is room for introducing simple, small changes to allow room for creative craft practice. Shaking up our daily rhythm will unlock a powerful reservoir of creativity within each of us. It just takes some small shifts in habit, and by simply changing certain patterns, it will allow opportunity for new experiences and give us the confidence and the right mindset to make more positive changes.

The value of *mini-c,* the deliberate act of creative activities (which we explored in Chapter One), is that it begins to open up different ways of thinking. Instead of performing the same tasks in the identical way we have always performed them, we should occasionally ask ourselves if it has to be done this way. You become more alert to where and how you might make small changes. Through these positive, manageable choices and routine re-jigs you can slowly gain a greater sense of control. Changing the way that you do things today will make an impact, hopefully positive, on your life in the future.

The Russian philosopher P. D. Ouspensky outlined the road to self-awakening, which, while rather esoteric, provides some interesting ideas on how we can begin to live more fully, be more perceptive and alive to the people around us and the evolving situations in which we find ourselves. If you begin to observe yourself in your interactions throughout the day, you increase a level of self-awareness which allows you to take part more fully in small daily decisions, as well as exploring new avenues of interest. This might involve taking time, for example, to savour the taste and texture of a crisp, sweet apple; to catch yourself when you are interrupting or are talking too much and you've lost the attention of your companion. Or when you begin to observe an obsessive thought circling round your head. If we are aware of these thoughts, but do not engage with them, they tend to dissipate. This awareness and inaction, in the same way we might focus on the breath during a meditation, helps to still our active minds. The idea is to bring your focus back to yourself, to understand you have the power to make changes and choices.

To some degree, we are all aware of the idea that stepping away from a problem, be it an aggressive email from a business partner or an uncomfortable exchange with a friend, can give us some perspective on how to resolve it. Rosemary remembers the best piece of advice she was given by a great boss, mentor and now friend, when she went to her with a problem. Her boss's advice was to 'lean on it' – not to act on the problem, but rather to let it settle. At the time, the advice seemed somewhat unsatisfactory – she would have preferred to be told exactly what to do and say to deal with it immediately, to shut the problem down. But she faithfully tried this approach. And it worked. Rosemary leaned on the problem and, within a couple of days, it had resolved itself. Without stress, endless emails and sleepless nights. Think how we might reflect on the greater challenges in our lives if we could also view them from an adjusted vantage point. *Lean on*, not in, the new mantra!

HOW TO SHAKE UP OUR ROUTINE

Neuroscience has shown that our brains seek novelty, that breaking out of some of our routines provides a little of that novelty, and inhibits distraction in our search for it. We all know how easy it is to become sidetracked when working at our desk, we are all familiar with the constant desire to flick between work, news feeds and social media, the relentless and ceaseless search for new information.

To shift our routines, we must, for a moment, step outside of them. This can be done on a very basic level where we choose to read a different newspaper instead of the one we turn to every morning. We can listen to more Ted Talks, read some non-fiction instead of fiction or vice versa. We could take a different route to work, play hide-and-seek with the children instead of making supper, start a daily diary, turn off our mobile phones for an hour or skip social media altogether, occasionally. We may choose to spend our lunch hour at an art gallery or go for a walk. None of these small adaptations to our routine is too onerous a first step in a lifestyle restructure.

The next step might be to flex your creative muscle further. The idea for 64 Million Artists was seeded when its co-founder Jo

Hunter had begun to feel unfulfilled in her work. She believed that she had to stay on top of everything in her life, that she had to aim for perfection to ensure nothing would ever go wrong. It was exhausting – there had to be more to life. Hunter took some time out of her job and in an attempt to shake things up, invited friends to set her a daily creative challenge: going for a walk with no destination; taking photos of all the blue objects she came across that day; writing a poem; making a drawing. She felt exhilarated by the tasks she was set and began to think about how everyone has a right to a creative life: that we are all instinctively imaginative but somewhere along the way, often via school and work, we have lost that connection. And while it's easy to lose touch with that side of our brains, it is also very easy to re-connect with it once again. Hunter set up 64 Million Artists with the ambition to unlock creative potential countrywide. The online daily crowdsourced challenges are not time-consuming, often only requiring ten minutes, while tapping into our creative potential.

While not making overarching claims that taking part in the everyday creative challenges will necessarily turn lives around, Hunter and her team found that participants felt more motivated and observant, enjoyed better confidence, but mainly they were engaged in just trying something new and seeing what happened.

Why not set yourself some daily or weekly creative challenges, or indeed sign up at 64 Million Artists. It is never too late to start a new hobby or return to a pastime you once enjoyed. The moment we allow ourselves to explore our creative impulses, many gentle and powerful changes can be expected.

A PRACTICAL APPROACH

The function of list-making is not solely for the pleasure of crossing off completed tasks. Making a list of pros and cons, feelings about a particular situation or possible resolutions to a troubling issue can take us directly to the heart of a problem. Consider the exercise of plotting out your entire day in blocks of work, responsibilities at home and leisure activities. These will change from day to day and you might see, very quickly, how to fit in an extra segment of time for a craft practice. Of course, it might mean that your leisure time looks different, but, given that you're reading this book, it shouldn't come as a huge surprise that you're being asked to tweak your routine!

Make a wish list of crafts you would like to try and some notes on how you might begin taking part. Is there a local class you could join to get you started? Books and videos are also great resources: do some research on the crafts that inspire you the most, regardless of their skill level. Remember, don't let a lack of belief in your creative abilities hold you back – all humans start from the same position of knowing nothing. Even the most skilled Japanese woodblock carver began by picking up a knife and following instructions.

Once your interests have been narrowed down, consider setting yourself a small challenge. Register for a workshop and learn a new skill: *by February I want to have bound ten pamphlet books; by March I want to print my first run of lino cuts.*

What are the obstacles in your life to starting a mindful craft practice? No time? Worried you might not be any good at it or are not the creative type? Are these real hurdles, or excuses to maintain the status quo, without disrupting the organised rhythm of your life? As we described earlier in Chapter Five, perfection isn't the goal and it might work for your lifestyle to have a rigid routine, but how much of it is genuinely enjoyable and makes a lasting impact on your mood?

SPACE

While everyone's dream is to have a room of their own, often this isn't possible. Not everyone has the luxury of a spare room for crafting or any other hobby. While this physical space doesn't have to be an entire room, it will be the place where you store tools and supplies. It may only be a small box to begin with. But there is an important step here in that when tools and materials have their own space and are within easy reach, they acquire a welcoming and motivating quality. They encourage your return to the pastime which gave you so much pleasure yesterday.

One school of thought promotes that preparation for any new home hobby begins with clearing out the jumble of long-dead projects and general clutter. Be honest with yourself about the value of keeping old junk around. There is a spring-cleaning quality to any decluttering activity and this is part of embracing a whole new lifestyle choice.

Marie Kondo, author of *The Life-Changing Magic of Tidying*, invented the term 'spark joy', a tool to help decide between which possessions to discard and which to keep. While taking hold of an item, such as a dress, a pair of shoes or a moth-eaten bag of wool scraps, we ask ourselves, 'does this spark joy in my heart?' and, if it doesn't, it's for the recycling. Kondo believes there we have an innate reaction to the items in our home, ones that 'spark joy' and the rest that don't. She asks you to imagine yourself living in a space that contains only items that 'spark joy'. It's a terrific image and one that, when,used consciously, encourages us not only to declutter, but to pause before we acquire new things. Do we really *need* another kitchen appliance or item of stationery? Don't we have enough stuff already?

Working in an inspiring environment stimulates creativity. Consider hanging a pin board with photos, postcards, samples of cloth, drawings – anything that ignites your particular creative impulse. Collect sources of inspiration, whether they're photos stored on your Pinterest or Instagram pages or magazines and materials in a folder. Surrounding yourself with your muse will help your practice thrive. Section off a stretch of bookshelf exclusively for your books of inspiration and crafting manuals.

Practical ideas might include using or buying a fold-down table that can be put away to conserve space in communal areas, or if you do have the space, consider cordoning off a corner of a room just for you and your supplies. A mobile drawer unit is incredibly useful for moving supplies around the house if you don't have the luxury of a dedicated space.

Embody your creativity by always having a pen and notebook to hand *wherever* you are. No one knows where or when the muse will strike.

'I started learning about ceramics about ten years ago; once I got my hands on the clay it felt like a calling. When I realised the possibilities of the medium, I was hooked and wanted to spend all my free time doing it. It became the release I needed; the more stressed I became at work, the more courses I signed up for.'
— *Ranjit Dhaliwal, picture researcher, potter*

Here are seven easy, effortless tips to get the creative juices flowing:

1. We love Etsy, Craftsy, Instagram, Pinterest and arts sites such as www.thisiscolossal.com (which we mentioned in Chapter Five) for ideas and inspiration (see p. 95).

2. Keep an ideas box into which found objects, scraps of material/old ribbons/recycled gems will nestle comfortably together until needed. Rifling through can sometimes spark an idea or an urge to make.

3. Treasure jars are similar to ideas boxes, but more suited to smaller jewels – beads, stones and pebbles, broken jewellery, ceramic chips, etc.

4. While out and about, get into the habit of using your phone to take photos of colours, buildings, materials – anything that catches the eye that might later be used to inspire your work.

5. Widen your horizons by visiting different and maybe more obscure art galleries and museums, locally or further afield.

6. Be mindful of consumption and expense by shopping around. Use eBay for bargains and cheap yarns, threads and other materials. Charity and secondhand shops can be a great source for yarn, knitting needles, reference books and old vintage fabrics. Flea markets can be a rich hunting ground for bargains, and street markets for stalls selling haberdashery, tools and kits.

7. Recycle and re-use: unravel old jumpers to make new woollens; use old clothing to make your first quilt or try some Japanese Boro patchwork.

Have a ball!

PART III

The Projects

"'There is no use trying," said Alice. "One can't believe
impossible things." "I daresay you haven't had much
practice," said the Queen. "When I was your age, I always
did it for half an hour a day. Why, sometimes I've believed
as many as six impossible things before breakfast.'"
– **Lewis Carroll**, *Through the Looking-Glass*

Whichever craft activity you take up, or think you might want
to have a go at, it must be enjoyable; it must deliver genuine
pleasure. Of course, there will be periods of frustration, but, until
you have mastered the basics, this is true of any new activity.

The drive to use your hands to make and create does not benefit
from over-thinking. Imagine you are playing, don't worry too
much about how it's going to turn out. To quote Picasso (again),
'To draw, you must close your eyes and sing.'

Do you like the idea of working with paper? Or are you seduced
by beautiful fabrics? Do you like precision and fine detail? Are
you good at measuring? Using a sharp knife? Have you always
wanted to write? Do you hate getting your hands dirty, or love
the idea of being elbow deep in paint or clay? Are technical

skills important to you or a more free-form approach? Try to remember what you enjoyed making as a child. This is a great place to start developing a sense of which direction you might explore.

Writing in the *Guardian* in 2017, NHS doctor Laura-Jane Smith describes how taking time away from work and rediscovering the crafts she had loved in her childhood helped in her recovery from a major depressive breakdown. Smith turned to knitting, drawing, writing, anything to challenge her brain in a different way, and felt recharged. And, on her return to work, continuing her craft activities has helped to make her 'a better colleague and a better doctor'.

> 'I like a mixed bag of craft activities so I'm really a jack of a lot of trades and definitely master of none. I do stained glass, am about to take up spoon carving and have my eye on a screen-printing course. Over recent years I have also tried silver ring-making and calligraphy.'
> — *Emma Smith, publisher, stained-glass designer*

Think about some craft or creative activities that will suit your particular skills and passions. If you already are a dedicated knitter, for example, why not step up to a new challenge and attempt a pattern you thought was way beyond your abilities. Stretching our goals is empowering – expanding our ambition by taking one small step can put us on track to tackling bigger challenges in our lives.

Whether you prefer to craft alone or within a group of likeminded makers, there are craft practices to suit every type of personality. Why stop at a single craft when there are so many to try and then to add to your repertoire of skills? Sometimes only a concentrated period of drawing will help shift the concerns of the day and at other times, only knitting or weaving will calm the mind chatter. Longer stretches of available time (and inclination!) lend themselves to printmaking or an intense period of pottering around the garden. Mix it up.

On this occasion, the internet is your friend. There is no technical crafting question that cannot be answered by a YouTube video; from the smallest query about the exact function of a bone folder to the larger question of exactly how to make a glaze for your newly thrown pot. These detours can be time-consuming, however, as one simple question can lead you to the further reaches of the internet, although along the way there is plenty of inspiration to be had from makers of the most obscure arts and crafts.

The projects featured in *Craftfulness* are to inspire further investigation into the world of craft. They are a sample of the crafts *we* are interested in, but are by no means an exhaustive list. While writing is not necessarily considered a traditional craft, we firmly believe (as editors!) that exploring ideas by putting pen to paper can induce the flow experience in exactly the same way as an hour's knitting.

We hope that some of the projects featured here appeal, but really the purpose is to stimulate interest. They are all easily accessible, require little specialist skill or tools, yet contain enough instruction to inspire further research. Use these short essays as a diving board into the deep sea of creativity.

BUILD A LOOM & WEAVE – *Arzu*

I was first properly introduced to weaving when my daughter brought home from school a simple project using wool oddments and a handmade cardboard loom. I was intrigued by the simplicity of the machine and the stunning effects from such a rudimentary tool using a blend of varied textures of wool, with very little skill required.

Encouraged by the relative ease of the loom's construction, I felt like this was a craft ripe for exploration. With some very basic woodworking tools (hammer and nails!) it needn't require a great deal of DIY skill to put together a more durable loom and from there it's a small leap to making a variety of looms of different shapes and sizes.

Weaving is an absorbing and highly creative practice and when the simple technique is mastered, it is an aspirational craft; the handweaver will discover the delights of different techniques using a variety of wool and thread and embellishments. The completed square or rectangle of weaving can be used for more ambitious projects, such as making a quilt. They can also be hung as works of art in themselves, as demonstrated below. Smaller weaves made on a mini-loom can be used to simply mend clothing, such as patches for the worn elbows of a favourite jumper or pair of socks. It is a perfect project to be enjoyed with children as it does not require great manual dexterity or hours of instruction.

There are many types of loom, from one of the most simple, which will be illustrated here, to the vast modern industrial power looms. Today handloom weaving is prolific. Pinterest and Instagram feature inspiring designs to whet the appetites of ambitious crafters. If you are new to weaving, this is a great place to start. Designing and making a compact loom are craft activities in themselves and little knowledge of woodwork is required.

This is a very basic introduction to weaving; there is a wealth of information available in either book form or on the internet featuring instructions for a variety of stitches, designs and styles. These simple instructions are a guide to making a loom, weaving a tapestry, removing and hanging it.

Using found blocks of wood or a discarded picture frame, small nails and a little patience, you are a few short steps away from making a permanent loom. This is ideal for using up scraps of wool or thread. Small looms are portable, making this an ideal activity for group crafting sessions.

Once you have mastered making a simple loom, you are a short step away from making looms of different sizes and shapes, as well as experimenting with varied thicknesses and textures of yarn. I have a number of round looms which I regularly use to weave elbow patches on worn jumpers.

THE PROJECT:
A weave for hanging on your walls

YOU WILL NEED

For the mini loom:

6 in x 12 in (15 cm x 30 cm) wood block
(or an empty wooden picture frame)
Ruler
Black marker pen and a pencil
Just under 1 in (25 mm) coppered hardboard panel pins
Hammer

For weaving:

Wool or cotton yarn
Scissors
Masking tape
Large needle
Emery board

THE BASICS

A *loom* is a device which interlaces threads to make fabric or a
tapestry. The *warp* is the long threads which are stretched into
place before the *weft* is introduced, and held taut. The weft is
the yarn which is drawn horizontally, over and under, over and
under the warp threads to create a weaving.

Very simply, the thread weaves in and out of the long strands.
Different weaving techniques can be combined to make unique
patterns of your choice, but here, we will focus on the building
of a simple loom and the *plain weave*.

THE METHOD

You can make your loom from any material substantial enough to withstand nails being hammered into it. I tend to source small blocks of wood from skips and offcuts from DIY projects, or old picture frames. I've also used some very thick cardboard tubing cut down into smaller hoops to make small circular looms.

The bigger your loom, the larger the finished weave. Weaving on much smaller blocks is admittedly a little more fiddly, but produces equally stunning mini tapestries.

The wooden block I'm using here is 6 in x 12 in (15 cm x 30 cm).

1. Using a ruler and pencil, begin by drawing a straight line about 0.5 in (1 cm) inside the top and bottom edges, as shown. Next, mark intervals of about 0.5 in (1 cm) along both lines. Start at about 0.5 in (1 cm) in from the edge, as shown.

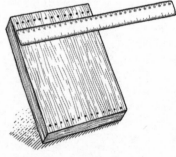

2. The nails I use are small panel pins – they need to have a head large enough so the yarn won't easily slip over and off the loom. Your local builders' merchant/hardware store will supply these in different sizes if you don't have them to hand. For this project I'm using just under 1 in (25 mm) coppered hardboard pins. Using your marks as a guide, gently hammer in the panel pins about 0.5 in (1 cm) apart. They don't need to go in too deep, but enough so they feel secure. Take care to keep the nails straight as you tap them in. For this size of

loom 13 pins will be used at either end.

3. Attach the warp threads: The warp thread is the yarn we lay vertically which will be interwoven with rows of the weft thread. First, attach your thread or wool to the nails on the loom to form the warp threads. I use a reasonably long length of a strong yarn for the warp as it needs to withstand the tension of being woven with the cross threads, i.e., the weft (you don't need to measure out the warp thread, it can just unravel from your ball). Again, if you don't have oddments of wool and cotton thread at home these are available at most craft stores.

4. Starting with the first nail, wrap the yarn around twice, leaving a long strand of just over 2.5 in (7 cm). Use a piece of masking tape to attach the spare yarn to the back of the wood block.

5. Then stretch the first warp yarn and loop it twice around the corresponding first nail at the bottom end – you want to create some tension in the warp yarn. Pull the yarn back to the top and loop twice around the second nail. Repeat until the block is completely threaded. Take care to keep the tension as you wind your wool up and down the length of the block. When you reach the last nail, wrap the yarn around it twice and again secure a tail of just over 2.5 in (7 cm) to the back of the block with the masking tape.

6. Now you're ready to start weaving! Here, you will weave four rows with one colour, as shown. First, measure out a yarn length of 35.5 in (90 cm) or approximately five widths of your block, plus 5.5 in (14 cm) to allow for just over 2.5 in (7 cm) tails at either side.

    (If you are completing even numbers of rows (2, 4, 6, etc.) for each colour then your dangling thread will always end up on the same side. If you are completing odd rows (1, 3, 5, etc.), then allow for 5.5 in (14 cm) extra thread (just over 2.5 in (7 cm) on each side). These can be taped to the underside, as before, or left dangling. In this project, I use an ordinary sewing needle, but have taken the step of blunting the sharp tip so it doesn't keep catching on the thread. I did this with an emery board, but you can use sandpaper or a nail file.

7. You will now weave in and out of the warp. Measure a space of about 1.5 in (3.5 cm) below the line of your nails: this is 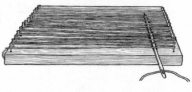 where the weaving will start. When your piece is finished, you will need to slip the loops over the nail heads, cut and tie them together. Guide the threaded needle through the yarn using an under and then over stitch: under the first stitch, over the second, under the third, over the fourth, and continue until you reach the end of the row. Now wrap the yarn around the last thread and guide your needle back along the row. This second row will be the reverse of the first, going under the first thread, over the second, and so on. Do not pull the yarn too tight as you make a new row, and take care to keep the warp threads straight.

8. As you progress it's important to gently nudge the rows together to ensure a tight weave – I do this using the needle.

9. To change to a new yarn colour, simply unthread the first yarn from the needle and tape or leave loose just over 2.5 in (7 cm) of thread, as before. The loose ends can be sewn into the back of the weaving when you're finished. Thread your needle with the new yarn and continue as above for the next row, as shown. You can also change yarn by knotting new thread to the old.

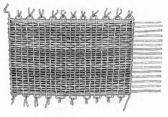

10. By the third colour change, the dangling threads at the side of your block may become a little irksome, so simply tape them to the underside of the block.

11. Continue to weave, changing your yarn colour every four rows, as shown. When you reach the top of the loom, simply peel off the pieces of tape and slip the loops off the nails. Snip in half the warp threads at the top and bottom of the loom and make double knots to secure the weave ends.

12. If you are not keen on the loose warp tassels, you can simply snip off excess yarn above the knot. Alternatively, the two long ends of thread at the top and bottom of your tapestry can be sewn through the back rows. Thread the loose ends with your needle, pass it to the back of the weaving and thread it through a few rows, then snip off the excess yarn for a tidy finish. Repeat this step with the excess threads from the weft rows, threading the yarn onto your needle, and passing it through the back of the weaving, as shown.

HANGING THE WEAVE

It is a simple enough process to hang the weaving now that you have mastered building your own loom.

1. Select a twig or wooden baton that measures just under 1 in (2 cm) wider on each side than your piece.

2. With the wrong side facing, thread just over 35 in (90 cm) of yarn through the top of your weaving and over the stick and back into the weaving to secure the thread and then make a small stitch still in the wrong side of your weaving, to define the size of your first loop, and secure it.

3. Now continue to thread through the tapestry and over the stick until you come to the end, where you will finish with another double knot to the back of the piece. Cut away the excess thread.

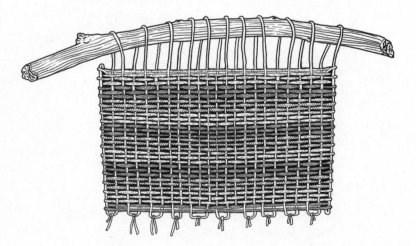

Voilà! Your weaving is ready for hanging on your wall.

KNITTING – *Rosemary*

'Properly practiced, knitting soothes the troubled spirit,
and it doesn't hurt the untroubled spirit either. When
I say properly practiced, I mean executed in a relaxed
manner, without anxiety, strain or tension, but with
confidence, inventiveness, pleasure and ultimate pride.'

– Elizabeth Zimmermann, *Knitting without Tears*

Of all the crafts, knitting is my bedrock, my go-to activity
which has seen me through some fairly dramatic ups and
downs over the years. I *love* it. I'm probably addicted to it – if
I don't have a piece of knitting on my needles, something is
definitely out of kilter. If I'm watching TV at home with my
children, more often than not, I will also be knitting. I *need*
to do something with my hands and knitting, for me, is the
perfect activity – I can be present, follow the programme and
conversation around me *and* knit a simple pattern.

I adore everything about knitting, from the textures of different
wools and yarns to the smell of those soft, warm bundles with
their paper belly-bands fresh from the shop. Wool shops draw
me to them like a magnet, their pigeon holes overflowing with
all those irresistible coloured balls of promise. And, more than
anything, I really like the buzz and nervous anticipation of
getting them home and casting on that first row as the needles
echo a very satisfying clicking and clacking soundtrack to
my work.

Part of the appeal of knitting is that it requires very little initial investment, just the two needles, the yarn and a pattern. I think it's great that it is a portable craft – as long as it's not an unwieldy blanket in its final stages, you can take your knitting with you anywhere. Finally, I love knitting because it is an eminently flexible, and quite forgiving, craft. Unlike dressmaking, where the seams have to be perfect, within a millimetre and neatly stitched, knitting allows quite a lot of room for error and manoeuvre – if you drop a stitch, with a little practice you can retrieve it, fix the problem and keep on going. If your jumper diverges from the pattern and one arm is slightly longer than the other, this also can be adjusted when sewing it up and finishing. As the wonderful Freddie Robins, textile artist and senior tutor for knitted textiles at London's Royal College of Art (RCA), says: 'With knitting you can tease it and shape it, it's a brilliantly fluid material.'

Knitting (once you've got the hang of it) involves working repeating patterns; there is a deeply soothing rhythm to the process – work a row, reach the end, turn around, and start all over on the next, and so on. It's hugely satisfying to watch the piece grow in your hands – to physically feel and see results in a relatively short time delivers such a sense of achievement and pride and drives the urge to keep on knitting.

It is also a perfect mindfulness practice. It is a rhythmic, hypnotic, deeply relaxing activity and once I start, I very quickly enter into a calm, focused place of flow. Even if I am with others, I can and often do go somewhere else in my head. Cups of tea go cold and undrunk, children become frustrated in their attempts to get my attention. Even when I am exhausted, I find it hard to stop – *just one more row, then I'll go to bed* – until, eventually, it really is the last row my sore eyes can manage when I force myself to stop.

We visited Freddie Robins, lecturer in textiles at the RCA, to talk knitting. Robins learnt to knit as a child and later set up her own textiles business before becoming an artist and tutor. She described how she turned to knitting after the birth of her daughter and subsequent postnatal depression: 'The process has to be enjoyable – the doing of it. If you're making work that takes quite a while to finish you have to enjoy the process. I value the well-being aspect – when my daughter was born knitting helped. The act of knitting, because I knew *how to do it* and had always knitted before my daughter was born, the physical act of doing it was calming and soothing.'

I no longer remember a time when I couldn't knit. My great-aunt Dolly, prodigious knitter and my instructor, was the inspiration, as I watched her day in, day out, busy at her needles to keep me and my sisters well stocked in fancy white acrylic cardigans and scratchy jumpers.

In my teens, I had a best friend with a very trendy older sister who introduced us to fashion magazines. Rural County Down, in the 1970s and 1980s, was not a great place for someone so quickly obsessed with the fashions found in the pages of *Honey*, *19* and later *Marie Claire*, *Elle* and *Vogue*. So there was only one thing to be done – I had to attempt to recreate some of the ideas on those glossy pages for myself. I didn't have the patience for sewing – I shrink in embarrassment when I think of one particular handsewn monstrosity I wore to our school prom – but knitting? That I could do! I was in my element with the arrival of punk and the mohair jumper, the looser and holier the better. Later, when I must have been around 15 or 16, I saw a model in a magazine wearing a cropped, cream cable jumper styled with a really cool, short kilt, Doc Martens chunky boots and holey tights – I remember my whole body flushed with yearning for that sweater. A trip to Belfast and its one and only department store, Robinson and Cleaver, supplied me with the perfect, soft, creamy Aran and, with some help, I mastered the cable stitch. And while it wasn't easy, I worshipped that jumper and wore it with the singular pride that comes from great achievement!

If you are a complete beginner and have never tried knitting before, it's not the easiest thing to teach yourself from a book. As Robins says: 'Knitting involves a lot of prep – it can be bewildering. It is a difficult skill which requires a lot of practice and learning, even the language of a pattern requires a knowledge.'

It really helps to have someone by your side to teach you the language when you are starting out. My advice would be to ask a friend, relative, neighbour or a local wool shop owner to guide you through the absolute basics: how to cast on; how to hold the needles and work the knit and purl stitches; how to read a pattern; how to retrieve the inevitable dropped stitch or two; and how to cast off. Start with something simple and achievable, like a scarf or knitted squares to make a small blanket. And stick at first to the basic stitches until you find your rhythm and gain a fluid movement and begin to feel yourself relax into the process.

Instructional videos on YouTube and online are a fantastic resource if you get stuck with a stitch or don't understand a new bit of knitting jargon in a pattern. But nothing beats that face-to-face, hands-on advice. I'm mildly dyspraxic and can still get muddled trying to follow the videos as it all looks back to front in my jumbled brain, so if I get really stuck I still pay a visit to the lovely Anna at my go-to wool shop with my knitting in hand.

It will probably feel slow, clumsy and a little frustrating at first, but like most things, including riding a bike, once you get the hang of it, you are off and running and you won't want to stop. You need to give it time and not give up too quickly before you have a chance to decide if knitting is really for you, or not.

It is good to know at this point perhaps that the starting of any wool project is the most difficult step. Finding the right pattern, working out which yarn to use, if the pattern will work with a different wool weight, which size needles are best for that particular yarn ... for years those were my main stumbling blocks. Even in London for a time there were very few places (aside from the department store John Lewis) where you could reliably find decent wool and someone on hand to help advise and order, if necessary, what was required. We are so lucky that knitting is popular once more and wool shops with passionate, dedicated, experienced staff have begun to spring up in many towns and cities. In my area alone, there are at least three good local shops within a short bus ride.

Always make a start on a new piece of knitting in the morning or part of the day when you feel fresh and the light is good – casting on and knitting the first few rows on any project are my least favourite part of the process. The casting on can go wrong if you are tired – if I cast on at night I can often catch myself in a loop of counting and recounting the stitches, and getting a different number each time. The first row of stitches are fiddly and, if I'm not relaxed, it's easy to make them too tight and tense, mistakes creep in and I have to unravel and start all over.

Knitting, like most things in life, can become an expensive hobby too if you are not careful. Making the decision to start a new knitting project can be as simple or as complicated as you make it, but it's always an investment in time and money. Wool and fabric shops can be gorgeous, but very costly, dens of temptation for overspending. Good wool is simply very pricey and sometimes difficult to resist if you want to make something special, but if I'm going to spend time and money knitting with fine wool, I find it reassuring to have someone to advise and guide, so that I know I'm on the right track. Don't be afraid to seek and take advice from experts. Good-quality materials are worth spending money on in the long run: you can indulge, but think about buying and supporting local wool manufacturing. Make considered, ethical choices where possible — and don't stockpile great bags of yarn that you may be unlikely to get round to using.

If you are still learning, use a less costly wool or cotton as you build your skills and confidence. It will be so much more relaxing and less stressful if you make mistakes and have to start over or ditch altogether early attempts. Begin by knitting a basic rectangle in garter stitch to make a scarf and gradually work your way towards learning purl. Combining these two stitches, where you knit one row, purl the next and repeat makes the stockinette, or stocking stitch. Before very long you will be attempting the patterned stitches: moss stitch, ribbing, cable stitch, and so on. Once you have the hang of these different stitches, buy and follow an easy pattern for a bobble hat.

THE PROJECT: KNITTING A SIMPLE SCARF IN MOSS STITCH

Knitted in moss stitch, this pattern makes a generously wide and pleasingly snug reversible scarf. For a narrower scarf, just cast on an even number of fewer stitches. Moss stitch is produced by alternating one knit and one purl stitch within a row — knit one, purl one, knit one, purl one and so on. Then on the reverse side, the knit stitches are knitted, and the purl stitches are purled. A knit stitch will look like a flat 'V' on the right side, a purl stitch forms a sort of rounded bump on the right side, so it's easy to keep track by simply looking at your knitting, and to alternate the knit and purl stitches without getting muddled.

When your scarf reaches the desired length, cast off in pattern for a neat finished end.

YOU WILL NEED
3–4 1.5 oz (50 g) balls double knitting wool
    (depending on desired length)
Pair size 0.2 in (4 mm or 4.5 mm) knitting needles
    (check the wool label instructions)
Scissors
Wool embroidery needle

THE METHOD
1.   Cast on 40 stitches using the long tail cast on method.

2.   First row knit one, purl one stitch to end.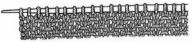

3.   Second row, do not knit the first stitch – simply slip it on to the right-hand needle. Skipping the first stitch in every row gives a neat side-edge finish.

4.   Continue to the end of the row in moss stitch, i.e., alternating knit and purl stitches.

5.   Continue to knit in rows until the scarf is the desired length, shorter for a neat little neck warmer, longer for a more sumptuous scarf that can be wound several times.

6. Cast off loosely and evenly in the moss stitch pattern – slip first stitch, knit/purl second stitch and slip second stitch over first, continue to end. On the last stitch,  cut the yarn and thread the loose end through the last stitch, pull gently to secure.

7. Tidy any loose lengths of cast on, cast off or joined yarn by threading on to the yarn needle and weave it through the wrong side of the scarf as neatly and invisibly as possible. Don't worry too much about small loose ends as these will shrink slightly and blend with the wool after washing.

8. Block the scarf, i.e., gently pull the fabric into shape lengthwise and widthwise, and steam with a cool iron.

9. Wear with pride.

'Craft has helped me to reclaim my power and I have never felt more secure in myself nor have I felt more capable of achieving my full potential. I have no doubt that this sense of empowerment is the direct result of the repetitive and melodic nature of knitting and the rhythm that develops between the eyes, hands and heart. Knitters have long acknowledged amongst themselves that knitting is an excellent form of therapy. It seems that science is now interested in establishing this as fact and I welcome the scientific community's interest. Knitting is mindfulness in action and extreme knitting is mindfulness at full volume.

I've never been able to quiet my mind in the way that traditional forms of meditation often require. As a result, for me the concept of mindfulness has been an enigma and its benefits elusive.

'I know through my experiences as a teacher of my process that many others feel the same way. The process of extreme knitting engages every part of me, allowing my unconscious mind to have a rest for a while. It's magic. Add the tactility, luxury and sensory delight of a beautiful natural fibre such as wool, and it takes the process to another level. Wool is a special ancient fibre that has provided humankind with warmth, comfort and protection for centuries. It has a rich and evocative beauty that is mesmerising, soothing and satiating. Its role in my recovery from what was a very difficult time in my life cannot be underestimated.'

— *Jacqui Fink, extreme knitter, fibre artist*

BOOKBINDING — *Arzu*

Within the pages of my handbound books I explore ideas and record thoughts which are often illustrated with simple drawings. These books tend to contain a mix of papers; plain, graph, lined and coloured pages jostle, shoulder to shoulder. Juxtaposing different textures and colours inspires the content; some pages will lend themselves to dense pages of text and others to pen and ink drawings. The craft of bookbinding is, for me, intrinsically bound up with writing and illustrating. It is an intellectual process, but resonates on a deeply emotional level because of the question each book asks: what am I for? Using my hands to make books which I then go on to fill with words and pictures is a contained and satisfying preoccupation.

Assembling paper and thread to make a book is an act of *intent* for me; the project isn't finished when I snip off the loose threads, if anything, it is merely the prologue to a story which is yet to be written.

Preparing the ground for binding a series of basic books begins with simple maths where I note measurements and then begin to think about the paper I will use for the covers and interior pages. By the time I am punching holes and cutting pages down to size, already the sense of excitement in starting a new project has taken hold. The intense concentration I feel is one of the traits of flow. It is pinpoint focus, a singular preoccupation which, for me, is particular to crafting. When I am this absorbed, I think of little else but the task at hand; it is almost like dancing, it feels completely natural: there is a rhythm to which I am responding instinctively and for a time worries about the past, concerns about the present and the future slip away.

I have found that this deep concentration almost negates the me who is sewing, cutting, sticking or drawing. Whether I finish the project in that session or have to return to it at another time makes no difference to my experience of total immersion. The more I develop my skills and the ease with which I move between the various stages of binding a book, the greater this sense of detachment from the world and attachment to the work in my hands. It is never easy to leave this absorbing state, but I have also found that the impression of such intense distraction lingers.

Bookbinding is a very tactile craft; besides exploring the different weights and textures of leather, cloth and paper, there is the singular pleasure of combining these materials to make a unique work and the huge satisfaction of holding the finished book in your hands for the first time.

There is a great deal of enjoyment to be had from selecting the right materials for the type of book you want to make, whether it's a journal, a scrapbook or a sketchbook. As I've waxed lyrical about earlier in this book, the preparation of materials, carefully measuring and cutting paper to size, then sewing together the pages, demands concentration and attention, but you are rewarded with a profoundly absorbing and satisfying occupation.

From the earliest scrolls in Ancient Egypt to the more contemporary handbound leather hardback, there are hundreds of different structures in between which continue to ignite the imagination of dedicated bookbinders. People have always found ways to make a record, whether it was on bark, parchment, bones or palm leaves, the history of the book is aligned with disseminating information. Bookbinding has a rich and intriguing history, well worth exploring. Adopting a craft that has such an empowering tradition connects the present with the past and the future.

Bookbinding is not confined to the act of sewing together loose pages, even though the sheer abundance of different structures provides enough inspiration for a lifetime; there is the dazzling array of equally compelling crafts associated with traditional bookbinding, such as marbling, paper-making, paste papers, sewing headbands, edge decoration, gold tooling, conservation and on and on ...

***

Spending an hour or so measuring and trimming sheets of paper, sewing together sections, attaching boards covered with decorative paper, pressing the drying book in a *nipping press* is absorbing on a very fundamental level. There is little time to ruminate when a precise series of tasks have to be performed in order to achieve the most pleasing results.

This makes bookbinding an ideal *flow* activity. Once a certain level of proficiency has been achieved the absorption in the process, the attention that is required when working on the fine detail, is all-enveloping.

'The excitement you get from writing or drawing for the first time – in a notebook, sketchbook or diary that you have made yourself – is greater than anything you'll get from a glossy shop-bought one.'
– **Sue Doggett**, *The Bookbinding Handbook*

Making a stitched pamphlet book

To make a 3-hole stitched pamphlet book using paper you have at home is a simple and satisfying exercise and might even lead to a lifelong passion.

YOU WILL NEED

Paper (four sheets of A4, one A4 sheet of decorative paper for the cover)
Ruler
Pencil
Craft knife
Needle
Thread
Tablespoon*
Cutting mat

THE METHOD

1. Fold in half the four sheets of A4 paper** (a mix of papers is great) to make eight pages of A5.

2. Using the back of the spoon, score each of these sheets along the fold to make sharp creases.

3. Insert the pages (*folios*) one into the other; this is called a *section* or a signature.

4. Using the ruler and craft knife, lay the section onto your cutting mat and, *carefully,* with fingers kept clear of the knife edge, remove 0.1 in (3 mm) of paper from top and bottom and side edges. The pages should now align evenly on all sides.

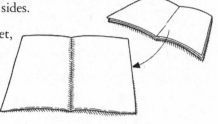

5. Remove the middle sheet, taking care to keep all the sheets in order, and lay it open on your workstation, spine fold down.

6. Along the spine fold, measure just over 1 in (3 cm) from each end and mark each point with your pencil. Measure the centre point between these points and mark this position as well.

7. Insert the sheet back into the middle of the section and set aside.

8. Fold and score the single decorative sheet and insert the signature.

9. Holding open the pamphlet, spine fold down, onto the mat board, make a small hole at each of the marks that you have just made. The needle must puncture all the sheets.

10. Thread the needle and, holding open the book with one hand, sew from outside of the cover up into the middle hole, leaving a tail of about 2 in (5 cm).***

11. Take the needle out through either of the holes at the end of the section to the outside of the cover.

12. Go back into the last hole at the other end of the section.

13. Take the needle back out through the central hole. You should now have two tails of thread together. They should lie either side of the long stitch on the outside of the cover.

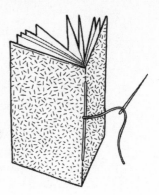

14. Tie the ends into a double knot and trim to the same length.

15. Score along the spine to consolidate the crease.

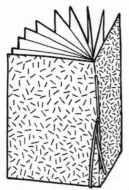

You have made a book!

*There are specialist tools which are inexpensive and well worth investing in should this be a craft you wish to pursue. They include a bone folder, waxed linen thread and a bodkin.

**Most manufactured paper has a grain. This allows the paper to be folded or torn more easily in one direction. You want the grain of the paper to run parallel to the spine of the book. To determine the grain direction, try gently folding the paper from edge to edge both ways. You will find more resistance against the grain.

***If you would prefer the knot to be on the inside of the pamphlet, start sewing from the inside of the section.

'Drawing is making, like making music, or planting
seeds, or chopping herbs and kneading dough. To draw
is to produce something which, however small, however
amateurish, never existed in the world before you made it.'
– **Andrew Marr, author of** *A Short Book About Drawing*

Drawing for me is very much a making practice. But before I
added it to my crafting repertoire, before I could rely on it to
deliver a *flow* state, before it became that moment of calm in
the storm of a busy day, I wanted to achieve a certain level of
competence. I desperately wanted to be that person who could
pick up a pen and translate on to the page, with a few brisk
strokes, any object or person who caught my eye. Whether it
was the profile of a friend or the campsite in which my tent was
pitched, the desire to draw was strong. But my skills were not
up to the mark.

So I had to apply a little discipline at the start of this particular
journey, so for a year, I drew every day. Most days, it was

the backs of my fellow commuters' heads on the top deck of the bus, on my way to work. I have sketchbooks featuring a proliferation of hoodies, shaved heads, curly hair. I made these drawings knowing I didn't have to show them to a single person. I could throw them away and no one would have to see these surreptitious scribblings.

My drawings steadily improved. And, very quickly, I began to enjoy trying. I look at these drawings now and they show me something I like, the side of myself that believes, 'if s/he can do that, I can at least have a go'. There is an undeniable freedom in drawing just for yourself, in a cheap sketchbook or on scraps of paper, with an ink pen. Even my 'bad' drawings had some value – if only to show a progression of skill, like a documentation of my journey.

When I eventually felt brave enough to show friends these commuter sketches, the feedback I received was overwhelmingly encouraging and enthusiastic. I may have chosen to believe they were only being kind, but instead I used this feedback to spur me on, to invest more time in drawing the things around me. I bought better paper and pens, added colour and researched the work of talented artists for inspiration.

Approaching a blank sheet of paper is a daunting prospect to begin with, but it is also exciting; it is the primary school urge to cover a pristine space with sharp black lines, soft pencil or creamy pastels. And often, in the early stages of reacquainting ourselves with drawing (we used to draw as very young children, remember?), it isn't until the figure or object comes into focus on the page that despondency may set in and the thought that this is a *bad* drawing discourages us.

The stark and simple truth is that to get better at drawing you must draw regularly. Few of us enjoy churning out bad drawings. But, in order to reach the point where the balance tips into being happier with our efforts, patience, self-belief and practice are key. Learning to draw is a journey that never ends, but it does have to begin somewhere.

Consider the obstacles that tend to get in the way of picking up a pencil day after day when we see no change in our abilities. The biggest hurdle is one's own lack of belief in the idea that with practice improvement is inevitable and the main reason we lose heart is impatience that we do not seem to be making progress faster.

Drawing and learning to draw cannot help but focus the mind and silence the nagging thoughts rumbling around our heads. When we begin drawing, our attention becomes fixed, and this spills over into the rest of our lives; we begin to see and note more of our visual world and what is going on around us, in nature, in our homes and in the streets. Very soon everything will become a drawing challenge; details you may not have previously registered hove into view, such as the different fonts and logos on condiment packaging, the many different greens that make up a single leaf, the texture of your children's skin.

Drawing is no longer the exclusive domain of fine artists. It has become largely democratised because of social media, where you can discover the work of an abundance of artists who have had no formal training, who are drawing just because they love it and want to do it.

Drawing is also not a gift endowed to some and not others. How you choose to develop your drawing skills will depend on who or what inspires you. Study the drawings of artists you most admire whose work makes an emotional impact – from Gwen John to Jenny Saville to the urban sketchers whose work on the internet is prolific and deeply encouraging.

For some, drawing is a deeply therapeutic pursuit. Like Danny Gregory, when his wife, Patti, became disabled, who said: 'Drawing definitely helped me then. And years later, when she passed away in a second accident, it helped me get through my period of grief. But drawing also helps me to navigate, sometimes literally. I always keep an illustrated travel journal when I go on trips, recording my observations and experiences in words and pictures.'

For broadcaster Andrew Marr, drawing helped him through the difficult recovery period from his stroke. 'I certainly didn't feel that I was myself properly until I found myself drawing again.'

ADVICE FROM THE EXPERTS

Danny Gregory has made a career out of inspiring his readers and students. His books are a wonderful testament to a life lived through art. He suggests that just as we learned to drive, we can learn to draw, as similarly no one was born a naturally gifted driver!

Gregory's commonsense advice for those new to drawing is pragmatic and encouraging ... and it actually works. Here are some tips from Danny himself:

- If you are just starting, chances are you haven't tried to draw since you were in school. You are rusty, but you are also, at best, still at the stage you left off, many years ago. Give yourself a chance to develop some skills. As broadcaster Ira Glass once said, when we begin a new thing our taste is far more advanced than our ability, so we tend to be very harsh in our judgement. But if we give it time, our drawing muscles will develop, as surely as if we were going to the gym each day.

- Don't start by looking around for a class to take. That's just an opportunity for procrastination. Just get a sketchbook and a pen and start drawing.

- Draw anything, then write a few words next to it, not about how crappy the drawing is, but about how you feel at this moment, what else is going on in your life, observations about this moment, what you smell and hear and sense about yourself. Use your drawing as a way to engage with the world around you.

- Don't judge your drawing. Instead of comparing it with your outsized expectations, try to enjoy the experience. Think of what you are learning about yourself. Give yourself time and a break, and just do it. Give yourself credit for trying. Judge later. *Muuuuuch* later.

Commit to just ten minutes a day; refer to the work of sketchbook artists for inspiration and, above all, enjoy the simple act of moving your pen or pencil over an expanse of blank paper to make your mark.

'For me, free drawing is a direct way to express conscious and unconscious motives. As a child, I was compelled to draw, I would turn to free drawing in an attempt to relieve a mood of anger or frustration or to indulge in reverie. In these moments, I found that the thin sharp pencil lines helped me express my feelings.'
– *Anne-Catherine le Deunff, art therapist, printmaker*

'Advice to people who want to start drawing? Buy a lovely sketchbook, ink pen. This will be your secret place, your special gift to yourself. Perfectionism is not required, make any mark, fill up that book, keep it a secret to yourself. Don't stop 'til you finish that book. Whatever is in your head. Nothing is wrong, no judgement. At the end of the book then ask yourself again what you think about drawing.'
– *Lisa Gornick, filmmaker, drawing*

Andrea Joseph, illustrator and blogger, has one last piece of very pertinent advice: 'Just do it. Just. Do. It. Stop over-thinking, stop judging yourself, just get on and do. The only way of making drawings that you're happier with is to keep on working at it. It's as simple as that, from my point of view. You can read and study as much as you like, but the only real way of improving your skills is by practice.'

Launch yourself in at the deep end by making a small drawing every day. Using a pencil or pen, whichever you prefer, draw objects around the house, such as cutlery, clothes, your breakfast, anything that stays still to start with. Gradually introduce colour, your pictures will start to come alive and serve as inspiration for more challenging subjects, or not – I continue to be perfectly happy drawing the packets and jars of food and condiments in the kitchen cupboards.

WRITING – *Arzu*

'Writing is medicine. It is an appropriate antidote to injury.
It is an appropriate companion for any difficult change.'
– *Julia Cameron, The Artist's Way*

Drawing and writing can be viewed as complementary well-being pursuits, and certainly, within the wide definition of craft in this book, we see them as making practices, bringing similar benefits to the creator. It is just as easy to lose yourself in a drawing as it is when writing a diary or piece of fiction or a comprehensive list of life goals.

However, writing may have a more direct therapeutic effect on mood and levels of stress. By being explicit in a piece of writing about events in our lives we are going straight to the heart of our problems, the core of our hurt, discontent or low mood.

One way I switch on and then off is to write at least one paragraph about any of the pressing thoughts on my mind. As well as encouraging reflection and focus, it also always surprises me that I have much more to say than a single paragraph. It's as though the act of writing spawns more writing, fuller disclosure, better insight. Opening up my notebook to a blank page can, occasionally, feel daunting, but with the first word, others flow and I can be writing for a good half hour with little awareness of the passing time. I have never shut my notebook feeling less positive, or more morose, and while it might not in itself resolve issues, it does give me some distance and a few moments to process what is at the heart of the issue.

The psychologist and author of *Opening Up: The Healing Power of Expressing Emotions*, James W. Pennebaker, conducted the most significant piece of research into the benefits of expressive writing, the results of which became known as the Pennebaker

Paradigm. In the late 1980s, he became interested in the impact of traumatic experiences on physical and mental health, and asked why is it that some people seem to deal with major upheavals better than others? He found that when people transform their feelings and thoughts about upsetting experiences into language, their physical and mental health often improve. Having any type of traumatic experience is associated with elevated illness rates; having any trauma and not talking about it further elevates the risk.

The results of his study showed that writing about a disturbing event for just fifteen minutes a day yielded significant benefits, which included an increase in psychological well-being and an overall reduction in visits to the GP. And most participants in the study reported that while they may have been initially upset by the experience of writing about their trauma, they acknowledged that the writing experience was a meaningful addition to their lives.

One idea which might explain why writing about our experiences, particularly traumatic ones, helps, is that it requires effort to suppress thoughts and feelings that might be uncomfortable, causing stress, psychologically and physically, and that by opening up and acknowledging what is going on in our lives by writing about it, we are reducing inhibition. Writing about difficult events allows us to make cohesive and coherent sense of them. It is a way of digesting our life experiences.

Whether we are familiar or not with the term *expressive writing*, the notion that writing is good for you has been supported through countless further studies and the fact that journalling and blogging is so prolific seems to point to its positive psychological impact.

Psychotherapist and author Kathleen Adams has actively pioneered the use of writing as a tool in therapy. Adams is also the founder of **journaltherapy.com**, where she advocates that keeping a diary or a journal is one way to stay in touch with our lives. It is about connecting with the present moment, as well as creating a bridge between the past and the future. Writing a journal can help us come to terms with traumatic experiences and aid the healing process by connecting us with our inner selves and our positive life events.

If keeping a diary is appealing then it is important to make a commitment to writing regularly, whether it is five minutes a day or three times a week or first thing in the morning. Just as with the other craft pursuits in this book, making the time and giving yourself the space will ensure you get the most out of the activity.

When we write about the events in our lives, we catch the delicate fleeting thoughts that we might otherwise dismiss. Writing is a way of making sense of what is going on and by venting our emotions or expressing frustration or joy it seems to make a positive impact on our well-being. Being able to untangle the knotty areas of a problem, whether it's within a relationship or work, helps us to see the issue more clearly, the many different strands that make up a problem, and make it easier to understand.

Objectivity is key to processing confusing or upsetting memories, but when such events are laid out for us to read on the page, the experience is translated into a kind of *mind map* of a small part of our lives. There is little as cathartic as pouring out your innermost fears or experiences onto a blank sheet of paper.

Whether one is writing a daily journal, being selective about the issues we want to explore or simply making a list of pros and cons, the effects on mental health are well researched. The proliferation of tools and advice to make expressive writing easy are abundant; whether we choose to write on our laptops, use a Bullet journal or simply a pen and notebook for a few minutes every day.

You may want to attempt Julia Cameron's 'Morning Pages' in *The Artist's Way*. The idea is that you write three pages in long hand, every morning, to navigate your way to greater creativity. The writing itself doesn't have to be about a particular issue, but anything and everything that comes to mind; small things, frustrating feelings, the hurdles in your path, your grand schemes. Don't think about what to write, just start writing, it's the exercise that matters. These pages are a way of spring-cleaning our heads of the messy jumble of thoughts, beliefs and feelings that might be holding us back, so that we can start our days fresh and thinking clearly. New ideas may come to mind, facilitating easier access to inspiration, the circling voices of doubt and self-judgement written out of the picture. These daily pages, which are most definitely private, can help to silence the inner critic and if it's creativity we are interested in, then the wisdom that comes with clarity of thought is much more accessible. Perhaps you'll find that if you keep writing, answers to the most knotty issues will eventually reveal themselves.

A regular writing practice can be part of our well-being toolbox for managing anxiety or coping with symptoms of depression. Identifying those areas of your life which continue to cause friction is the first step on the path towards finding a resolution and thus reducing intrusive circular thinking, which leads nowhere and often hijacks any notion of a destination.

Adams's advice to novice journallers is to not impose too many rules on how much or how often to write. For some, ten minutes a day works and for others, two or three times a week.

As a tool for documenting episodes from your life, your journal should be a robust documentation of significant moments featuring enough detail to encourage reflection in order to be able to process events. It needn't be a linear record of day-to-day events, but rather only those that have made an emotional impact.

The morning pages are a great place to start this journey, but equally, writing about the things going on in my life seems to untangle my thoughts and helps to make me feel more in control of whatever episode I'm discussing. It can be a revelatory exercise if you're honest and expansive and, at the very least, it can help you to pinpoint your own deep feelings around an area of concern or celebration.

CLAY – Rosemary

Although I have always wanted to try my hand at ceramics, I've been learning pottery for only about a year. I can pinpoint the exact time in childhood when I first had the desire to have a go – perhaps I'm one of countless viewers of BBC1's *The Generation Game* who watched Brucie and Anthea set some hapless contestants the challenge of making a pot on a wheel with fairly hilarious results. That was the moment the seed was planted.

With my friend Cath and two fellow beginner potters, every Saturday morning we convene in a back garden shed with local teacher Joanna. For a long while, my lessons focused on experimenting and playing with the many different types of clay and glazes, and concentrating on handbuilding techniques from the basic pinch pot and coiling, to rolling the clay and slab work or using moulds.

The minute I sit down with a lump of clay on the table in front of me, I'm like a child again, happy, excited and questioning. What, I wonder, could I make today? But before we get started there are things to catch up on, stories to tell, updates on our lives and work.

While we are talking, laughing and sometimes sounding off, the clay begins to take shape in our hands. Holding and turning a ball of clay in my hand to warm it through, I stick my thumb in the middle and start to gently shape and pinch it, I look down and see the beginning of a bowl in my palm. The direction and size of the vessel or bowl it will soon become is up to me, but the feel of it and basic shape of it moulded itself through touch as we talk. I can leave it largely as it is, a small pinch pot. Or I can begin to hand-roll coils of clay to start building it up, shaping and smoothing it as the pot grows. When it has reached the form and size that fits, we leave it to partially dry, or get to the leather hard stage where the clay is strong enough for patting with a paddle to add a different angle, or reshape it. Then the following week, it's time for smoothing and perfecting or burnishing the surface of the clay with a kidney-shaped tool made of flexible steel or stiff rubber, or for adding texture and pattern.

As a novice, having other potters around as well as our teacher is crucial – we watch each other's work in progress, exchange or borrow each other's ideas, and improve as we learn. On some mornings, I feel a liberating silliness, an urge to make something completely for its own sake, and not really worry about the results, whether it's a conventional shape or a functioning piece, such as the pinch pots described on p. 158. The joy of clay is that if your piece is not working out, it can be scrunched up, kneaded and reworked.

For all its immediacy and intuition, there is a lifetime or several, infinite lifetimes of skill to be learned in handbuilding with clay. Without getting too mystical, it is a timeless art that somehow embodies time. Working with just your hands and the clay on a handbuilt piece slows down time in the process. Unlike throwing pots on the wheel, building up a pot with coils or rolling out and shaping a plate or platter by hand can take as long or as little time as you choose, but at the least several weeks' worth of Saturdays, or more. How long you continue to work a piece comes down to instinct and personality and there is often a point at which you know or learn when to stop – when, for me at least, to continue to attempt to make something perfect will only make it more imperfect.

'Pottery is a skill that takes years to learn but is a craft from which you can gain instant satisfaction, just in the making and doing. There's a mystery to pottery, especially when you are a relative novice as I am. Applying glazes and the nuances of the firing process means you can never entirely predict how your work will come out. It's addictive. The more I do, the more I want to do.

'When I began pottery lessons, my friend and I would be at total odds with our teacher, a self-employed potter of many years. We'd arrive loud, out of breath, full of the day's anxieties. She taught us to slow it down, not to be obsessed with output. That the enjoyment of a lesson wouldn't be in finishing as many pieces of pottery as possible. It's a slow process, full of stages that can't be rushed. Our teacher works alone and there needs to be a kiln's worth of work in order for a firing to happen. One bowl might take six or seven weeks to emerge and that's just the way it is.'

— Chloe Healy, marketing director, potter

Working with clay seems to fit my personality and my abilities, perhaps because it's quite a forgiving, *wabi-sabi* material. Unlike Arzu, I'm not so good on precision and neat, sharp edges. I'm drawn to the supple, *roundedness* of the feel of the clay in my hands and of the soft forms and finish of the objects made with it. While the clay is still wet and malleable, if a coil-built pot starts to lose its shape and get too baggy, you can usually fix things: cut out a triangle of clay, score, rejoin and smooth the join. It's like cutting pastry to fit a pie dish, wet clay can be trimmed and moulded and smoothed back seamlessly into shape.

Working with clay is a stilling, regressive, playful experience. Getting your hands dirty, the smell and feel of wet clay between your fingers, the earthy grit under your fingernails takes you right back to the days of mud pies and the sandpit. The time you can spend lost in smoothing and burnishing, in the painting and glazing, ticks all the mindfulness requirements. At a certain point during the lesson, the chatting stops and we are lost in the work and in our thoughts, that's the magically therapeutic and soothing element of this craft.

Then there's the sense of achievement, surprise and the joy of arriving to find a finished pot glazed and sometimes still warm from the kiln. The unpredictable mystery of the glazes, how they react with the clay, with each other and with the heat of the firing never loses its element of wonder. There is pride and delight, sometimes disappointment, frustration or sadness when a piece comes out cracked or the hoped-for colour of the glaze finish is not at all what you expected. And sometimes it's the imperfections and mistakes that make the finished item unique, not necessarily ideally aesthetic, but special. That's all part of the *wabi-sabi* joy of working with clay.

If you are already a practised potter, you will understand the mindfulness benefits of working with clay. Perhaps partly due to the recent BBC *Great Pottery Throwdown*, the popularity of pottery and ceramics is on the up and up and it seems to be easier than ever before to access classes and studios. If you've always had a yearning to try your hand at ceramics, now is the moment to book a pottery class.

'Learning a new craft is such a feel-good activity and a class environment where you can meet new people somehow enhances that "good feeling". From my first pottery class I was totally hooked. Working with clay is very tactile – in some respects it's a deceptively simple activity with a beginning and an end to it that anyone can engage with, but it does require a surprising amount of focus and concentration; it's not something you can do half-heartedly. For those two and half hours nothing exists except for that lump of clay in front of me; I am solely concerned with shape, structure and texture. Time seems to stand still and whatever else is going on in my life stays outside, doesn't come into the classroom – without exception everyone comments on how de-stressed and relaxed they feel after each class. I seriously think most businesses would benefit from employees having access to a pottery suite: just fifteen minutes playing with a lump of clay, making a pinch pot, can disentangle your brain.'

– Cara Gordon, fine artist, potter

It took me four decades to get round to finding a teacher and booking classes, and I have only very recently started to throw on a wheel, which is proving both challenging and very satisfying as I stretch myself to get the hang of it, but such is life and full-time work and children, better late than never to finally realise that childhood ambition. And now that I've started, I suspect that I will be potting into my old age.

THE PROJECT:
make a clay pinch pot

This is the simplest and most instinctive way to make a small pot or bowl, and probably the first exercise of any student potter. Most Japanese Raku tea bowls were and still are made using this method, and although your first attempts may look a little, ahem, primitive, with some practice delicate and beautiful pots

can be achieved in a very short time. According to the great
father of British craft pottery, Bernard Leach, 'with practice,
bowls about the size and shape of half a coconut, but thicker
than a coconut shell, can be made in five or ten minutes without
any scraping or cutting'.

Most art and craft shops will have a number of air-drying clays
to choose from, so this is a simple enough exercise to try at home
(I use Fimo modelling clay, which dries in 24 hours). These
pinch bowls need to be made fast and instinctively and don't
require over-thinking or over-manipulation.

The whole process should take no more than around ten minutes –
any longer and the clay will start to dry and split –
if that happens, you can moisten your fingers slightly with water,
but not too much or the clay will get too wet and soft
to work with.

Tip: If your fingernails are long, you might want to trim them
before attempting the pinch pot.

YOU WILL NEED
1 packet of air-drying clay
Cloth or tea towel
Acrylic paints
PVA glue or clear acrylic varnish
Paintbrush

THE METHOD

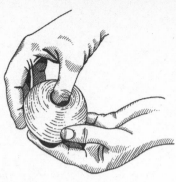

1. Take a small ball of clay, about the size of a tangerine, and round and smooth it in the palm of your left hand (or right if you are left-handed).

2. Hollow out a cavity in the centre of the ball with the thumb of your right hand.

3. With the clay gently cradled in your left palm, proceed to use your right hand's fingers to make the wall of the bowl thinner by squeezing and pressing gently against the thumb inside with a regular pressure as you work round the ball in a quiet, slow spiral movement. While working, I tend not to look at the work in my hands, but simply try to feel the width of the wall in my fingers and gradually get a feel for where the clay might need an extra gentle pinch to achieve an even wall width.

4. Within a few minutes you should have a small, fat bowl of about 2 in x 2 in (5 cm x 5 cm) in your hand. Start again to pinch evenly around the entire outer surface of the bowl with the tips of the fingers at the bottom; this time, the squeezing needs to be closer and more even to achieve a smooth surface. At this stage the thickness of the bowl in the lower part should be no more than is finally required – but don't be tempted to try to make the wall too thin or the sides of the bowl will simply flop over and collapse. Try not to pinch or mark the soft clay with your fingernails.

5. As the bowl grows a little bigger and the walls thinner, continue to support it in the hollow of your left hand held at an angle while you continue to gradually squeeze or gently pinch the clay up the wall with a gathering movement of the fingers.

6. Gently place the finished little pot on its base on a piece of dry, clean cloth or a tea towel and leave to air dry according to packet instructions.

7. When completely dry, the pot can be decorated using acrylic paints, and covered with a clear varnish or PVA for a glazed gloss effect to finish.

'I'm not a classic potter as I don't use a wheel.
I primarily use a buff stoneware clay to fashion bowls that look like leaves and candlesticks that look like dead trees. The sculpting is more fun than making bowls but also more effort. Bowls require very little thought – I can just be and let thoughts flow.

'Clay is soft. It is wet. It is malleable. It moves and responds to your hands in a way that wood or fabric does not. It is mud pies for grown-ups. My pottery shed is a place I can be calm and alone without loneliness. And it's fun. Really fun. I sometimes make little animals or gnomes and amuse myself by giving each one a different expression. The joy of bringing something from nothing. *Start with a lump, end with a fairy-tale creature.'*
– Katherine Kingsford, writer, potter

MENDING & DARNING - *Rosemary*

Of all the benefits to becoming a more capable crafter, for me, the most useful or gratifying aspect is not necessarily or always the ability to make *new* things, but having the wherewithal to mend the things that I already own. I'm not talking about major mechanical, plumbing or electrical repairs, or, in my case, even simple DIY jobs. But, as a knitter and sewer, the area where I can come into my own is in making small repairs to everyday items and clothing.

I've recently made a resolution to place an embargo on any new purchases for at least six months – to make more effort to curb splurging and to be happy making do with what I have, which is already enough. I find it hard to part with things that are damaged or imperfect, instead setting myself goals to mend, glue, reuse and repurpose. And when I eventually get around to it, I am an inveterate and enthusiastic, if not perfect, *fixer*. The second part of this resolution, therefore, is to fix things *sooner,* and to get better at the *art* of mending.

Undoubtedly, making something from scratch has the thrill of possibility and novelty, of innovation, as the blank page, the fresh ball of wool and the lump of clay patiently await the maker's magic touch. By contrast, a pile of mending has the whiff of housework about it. The collection of cracked bowls and handle-less cups, the snapped plastic fridge divider lurking in a corner of my kitchen; the growing pile of holey jumpers, fraying hems, my offspring's trousers in need of a tuck or a button, has

less the tendency to spark joy and more a scowl of reproach.
But, seen in a different light, there is an art to mending and,
approached in this frame of mind, it can be just as creative and
fulfilling as making an object from scratch.

VISIBLE MENDING

Invisible mending on most objects is almost impossible to achieve.
This is probably the first and most important point about repairs
and darning. A bowl once smashed in two will show the crack,
however infinitesimally small. Once a garment has lost its pristine
newness, all the patience and skill in the world will not magically
repair a tear. The point here is to accept the tear, the break, the
hole, the rip, apply patience and care and you might find that
the repaired item becomes even more beloved because of the
investment of your time and skill to make it *whole* again. Or take
inspiration from visible mending artists Celia Pym and Tom of
Holland, who both make a bold and colour-rich feature out of
centuries-old darning techniques.

The *wabi-sabi* approach of the Japanese mending arts is a rich
seam of inspiration for repairs around the house. For fabrics,
Sashiko stitching is used to reinforce and strengthen thinning or
weak areas of cloth, similar to the technique in Indian Kantha
fabrics, where old saris are layered and patched together, then
oversewn with a visible cotton running stitch; jeans and sheets
and any cottons or linens can be transformed using beautiful,
rustic Japanese Boro patching techniques.

With crockery, the *Kintsugi* technique favours visible mending when it comes to chips and cracks, thus making a virtue of the damage. *Kintsugi* means 'golden joinery' or 'to patch with gold', using gold with lacquer or epoxy glue to enhance these breaks and cracks, giving the broken pottery a whole new lease of life.

Once we embrace the creative possibilities in fixing things, and let go of the notion of the perfect, invisible mend and the worry that our repairs will render the crack, dent, vent, tear or moth hole even uglier, mending becomes a much less stressful, much more enjoyable process.

DARNING

Darning techniques have a long tradition, skills passed down from grandmother to mother to daughter down the ages. In the past woollens and stockings would have been hand-knitted and made to last. Clothing and garments were precious because they were either made by hand in the home or ordered to measure and made bespoke by a seamstress. In most households, therefore, mending and repairing were a necessity. During the Second World War, and in the time of austerity and rationing, the Board of Trade issued leaflets on every aspect of household management, from recipes for leftover food scraps to darning advice – it was the patriotic duty of the nation at war to do their bit for the war effort. 'Make do and mend' became the motto of the age, while government directives made darning the duty of every patriotic housewife.

For many of us today, though, darning and mending is a lost art – these age-old skills skipped the generation of our mothers, for whom the fight for equality and for feminist ideals meant a rejection of and disinterest in the domestic. Happily, today, feminism and a can-do attitude to mending no longer need be mutually exclusive and we can equip our sons and daughters to be proud and handy with a needle and thread.

'A neat darn is a real badge of honour these days – and done in good time it can lengthen the life of a garment by months and months.'
Darning Dos and Don'ts, The Board of Trade

The original 'make do and mend' pamphlets by Mrs Sew and Sew are available in a facsimile edition and are still a source of sound advice and instructions for darning and mending. For the modern mender, keen to minimise waste and counteract the throwaway culture of consumption, these handy tips are worth bearing in mind:

Don't:
- delay darning jobs – mend a hole or thinning area as soon as you spot it
- use a mending thread too heavy or too fine – try to match the yarn fabric
- make straight edges to your darn; a little irregularity distributes the strain

- pull the thread too tight or it will leave an unsightly pucker

- expect the mend or darn to be completely invisible – even the neatest darn will probably be noticeable

- expect to make a success of a job by hit-or-miss methods (!)

Do:
- darn on the wrong side

- darn as soon as a thin place appears in the fabric

- baste a piece of netting on a large hole and darn across it for extra strength in the weak area

- darn at least about 0.5 in (1 cm) beyond the hole or weak point

- leave small yarn loops at the turns to avoid puckers and to allow for shrinking of the darning yarn

- make yourself comfortable and in a good light before you start your mending

- embrace and accept a little imperfection in your mended garment or make a virtue of it through visible mending methods

If your woollens have been subjected to the occasional moth midnight feast, mending holes in knits is probably the most useful darning technique to master. There is an absolute truth to the cliché *a stitch in time saves nine* – if you notice a tiny moth hole or a thinning patch at the elbow of a sweater, mend it immediately.

If moth larvae are the cause of the damage, firstly place the garment in a sealed plastic bag and put it in the freezer for a couple of days, then remove and air the garment, allowing it to return to room temperature. The freezing process should then be repeated – this should kill any eggs and moth critters that might still be hiding out. With tiny holes you are more likely to achieve a pleasing mend if you use a yarn to match the weight and colour of that of your woollen. If not, find the closest matching thread, and if you are still keen to make an invisible mend on a small repair, choose a shade darker than the original, as lighter colours tend to show up more.

THE PROJECT:
Classic darn technique

The simplest way to understand this method of darning is to think of it as weaving – as in mini-loom weaving featured on p. 119. The aim is to replicate the original stitch or weave of your garment's knit or fabric as neatly and consistently as possible, so the yarn is simply woven over and under weft threads to fill the damaged hole.

YOU WILL NEED

Embroidery needle – match the size of needle to the fabric you are mending – a very fine wool requires a fine-pointed needle, larger knits will need a bigger blunt-ended needle

Yarn – in a weight to match your garment, either in a matching or a contrasting colour

Darning mushroom (or embroidery ring)

Scissors

Cotton tacking thread

THE METHOD

1. Working on the wrong side of the garment, place a darning mushroom (you can use anything with a rounded side – a light bulb, a lemon or plastic bowl) under the hole. For mending a hole in a flat piece of fabric, an embroidery ring will help to keep the garment taut and the darn flat.

2. Use cotton tacking thread to sew a circle of running stitch about 0.2 in (5 mm) away from the edge of your hole – this is to prevent the hole from stretching and unravelling while you are mending it.

3. Secure your darning yarn by sewing two or three small, neat stitches on top of each other, in an undamaged part of fabric close to the hole. (On thicker woven fabrics, you might be able to do this without stitching all the way through to the right side.)

4. Sew vertical stitches across the hole starting and ending close to, but on the hole side of, your circle of running stitches, keeping the end stitch on either side with a little bit of slack so that it forms a slight loop, as shown – this is to allow for shrinking of the woollen darning yarn. Don't be tempted to pull the stitches tight across the hole you are mending as this will cause a pucker in the fabric.

5. Next, weave a series of horizontal stitches perpendicular to your vertical stitches, working the thread over and under the vertical stitches to fill in the hole you are mending.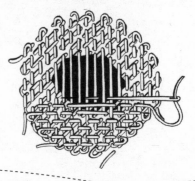

6. To finish, turn the mend over and pass the needle back to the wrong side, and weaving the thread into the back of the repair, make two or three small finishing stitches to secure. Snip the excess thread and there you have it!

DARNING KNITTED GARMENTS

With knitted garments and socks, the darning technique follows the instructions for the classic darn in the illustration on pages 167–8, but the second set of stitches used in the weave are made on the diagonal, as shown in the illustration. This is to allow for movement and stretch in the knitted yarn, similar to the concept of a fabric cut on the bias to fit.

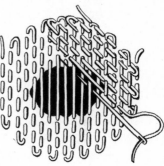

A small hole can be filled neatly using a yarn in a lighter weight to the garment, as described already. But for areas of larger damage, where an elbow has completely worn bare or there is a large gaping hole, a neat invisible mend will be an impossibility. This is the perfect opportunity to make a feature of the visible darn.

Experiment with darning techniques to make a feature of the mends – use contrasting colours and a different type of yarn, play with embroidery stitches.

Epilogue

As keen bookbinders, knitters, printmakers, etc., craft is woven into the very fabric of our daily routines, much in the same way we work or manage our households. These pastimes are an intrinsic part of our lives; they would be very different lives without wool, paper and ink. Articulating just what impact craft makes on our mood and well-being takes some unpacking. It is not a linear path to happiness; happiness evolves (and sometimes dissolves) by degrees and it is only when deconstructing the elements of a balanced life, filled occasionally with true contentment, that we can look at, for example, the practice of binding together blank pages to make a simple book, and think, 'this feels so good I want to do it again … and again.' And thereby take away the idea that doing things that make us feel good is good for us.

One of the moments of pure revelation for both of us came with the realisation that it doesn't matter which craft you pursue, the benefits are equally deployed. As you'll have worked out by now, while Rosemary is drawn to needlecrafts, to the soft textures of material, the bounce of wool, the soothing click of wooden needles, this suggests she is comfortable with crafts that are forgiving, highly adaptable, imprecise and fluid. If a jumper takes an unusual turn she can, with some effort, either retrace her steps or bury the problem with some clever needlework. Arzu is at home with the technical, with millimetre precision, perfect registration, sharp corners and maths, crisp sheets of paper, the razor edges of Japanese woodblock knives. We are, if you like, the yin and yang of our crafting world, each of our areas demanding different skills but the same focus.

When we began to discuss the idea for this book, we made a list of all the makers in our community. By *community*, we mean, very simply, our friends who regularly craft. Friends with whom we discuss craft (obsessively), collaborate with (occasionally), and craft together (companionably). The list delivered a rich collection of craft activities and enthusiastic makers.

We asked each maker the same six questions. It may be that they were leading questions; the method of interview certainly wasn't scientific, but the answers we received, time and again, were accompanied by a passionate acknowledgement that, somehow, in thinking about their responses, their process, the maker was, in turn, moved, absorbed, intrigued and reassured by the answers they delivered.

Many, up until then, had not put into thoughts or words exactly what role their craft activity played in their lives; many had underestimated its significance or not considered its general impact on their lives *at all* – and it wasn't until asked specifically what pottery or knitting or quilting meant to the maker that heartfelt and moving words poured forth.

For some, craft had helped with grief, others mild depression, but for all of them there was recognition that craft was as natural and essential a part of their lives as eating or sleeping. Many of our makers reported the interview experience to be *cathartic* – a revelatory 'so that's why I do it' moment.

Here are the questions. If you are a seasoned crafter, or even new to a craft practice, you may enjoy answering them. Be *honest* and expansive, we won't be chasing you for your feedback, but we think you might find this a useful and very pleasing exercise – never underestimate how a creative and enjoyable craft activity can enrich your life and make you feel good.

1. What job do you do?

2. What is/are your craft/art activities?

3. What motivated your interest in this craft? What is your motivation now to keep at it?

4. How do you fit your craft into your life?

5. In as many or as few words as you like, tell us how you feel while you are making.

6. What, if any, are the wider benefits or lasting effects of having a craft practice?

And, just in case you're interested ...

CRAFTS PURSUED BY ARZU

Drawing
Bookbinding
Weaving
Japanese woodblock printmaking

CRAFTS PURSUED BY ROSEMARY

Knitting
Ceramics
Wood engraving
Mending and darning

These are the crafts we found ourselves naturally drawn to, but we dabble and delight in many, many others. Some weave in and out of our established routines and others make guest appearances according to mood and inspiration. But, whichever you choose to have a go at, the message is the same: making time to make things is good for the soul.

References & Sources

RECOMMENDED READING
AND BIBLIOGRAPHY

It's Not How Good You Are, It's How Good You Want to Be, Paul Arden.

The Embroidery Stitch Bible, Betty Barnden.

The Creative Cure, Carrie Barron and Alton Barron.

Drawing with Children, Mona Brookes.

The Artist's Way, Julia Cameron.

How to Be a Craftivist, Sarah Corbett.

Happy, Fearne Cotton.

The Case for Working with Your Hands, Matthew Crawford.

Shop Class as Soulcraft: An Inquiry into the Value of Work, Matthew Crawford.

Flow: The Classic Work on How to Achieve Happiness, Mihaly Csikszentmihalyi.

The Bookbinding Handbook, Sue Doggett.

Happiness by Design, Paul Dolan.

Drawing on the Right Side of the Brain, Betty Edwards.

Arts in Health, Daisy Fancourt.

Made by Hand, Mark Frauenfelder.

Making Is Connecting, David Gauntlett.

Making Handmade Books, Alisa Golden.

Everyday Matters, Danny Gregory.

An Illustrated Journey, Danny Gregory.

Let Me Out, Peter Himmelman.

In Praise of Slow, Carl Honoré.

The Life-Changing Magic of Tidying, Marie Kondo.

Wabi-Sabi, Leonard Koren.

Why We Make Things and Why it Matters, Peter Korn.

The Drawing Book, Tania Kovats (editor).

Finding Your Zone, Michael Lardon.

Hands: What We Do with Them – and Why, Darian Leader.

The How of Happiness, Sonja Lyubomirsky.

A Short Book About Drawing, Andrew Marr.

Drawing Projects, Mick Maslen and Jack Southern.

The Happiness Project, Gretchen Rubin.

Option B, Sheryl Sandberg and Adam Grant.

The Craftsman, Richard Sennett.

Together, Richard Sennett.

A Field Guide to Getting Lost, Rebecca Solnit.

Playing and Reality, D. W. Winnicott.

INSPIRATIONAL WEBSITES

http://meetmeatthealbany.org.uk

Meet Me at the Albany is an all-day arts club for the over 60s, quite unlike anything that has come before. Based at The Albany, an arts centre in Deptford, south-east London, an all-year programme of weekly events creates opportunities for people to meet new friends and try out a whole range of new activities and experiences.

http://www.twistcollective.com

Independent online magazine focusing on knitting and the sister arts.

https://www.selvedge.org

Selvedge magazine and source of inspiration for designers and devotees alike, the Selvedge brand has flourished not only into a spring-board for makers and artisans, but also a strong community of textile lovers, with workshops, fairs and its own store.

http://celiapym.com/

Celia Pym is an artist, specialising in knitting, darning and embroidery.

https://tomofholland.com

Tom van Deijnen is a self-taught textiles practitioner, based in Brighton, UK. He works mostly with wool and has workshops and holds events.

http://malepatternboldness.blogspot.co.uk
The site of blogger New Yorker Peter Lappin, who specialises in sewing. Includes projects, sew-alongs and tutorials.

http://www.textielmuseum.nl/en/current-expositions
This textile museum is based in the Netherlands and has exhibitions and events.

https://www.thenewcraftsmen.com/handmade-craft-makers
The New Craftsmen has a network of over 100 British makers and works to refine and redefine the value of craft through curating, commissioning and selling their work.

http://www.thisiscolossal.com/
Colossal is one of the largest visual art, design and culture blogs on the web. Celebrating the work of both established and emerging artists across a vast field of creative endeavours, featuring more than 5,000 articles on fine art, crafts, design, animation, photography, street art, illustration and architecture, it reaches an audience of 2–3 million every month.

http://fuckyeahbookarts.tumblr.com/
A blog for creative types interested in the (un)conventional world of book arts! Featuring artist's books, illustration, bookbinding, typography, sketchbooking, scrapbooking, printmaking, papermaking, altered books, how-to guides, zines, paper engineering and more, fuckyeahbookarts is wildly inspirational!

http://bigjumppress.com/home.html
An inspirational blog by Sarah Bryant, featuring her letterpress
printed artist's books, prints, broadsides and handbound books.

http://thisisnthappiness.com/about
A brilliant tumbler account featuring 'art, photography, design
& disappointment'.

http://tommykane.blogspot.co.uk/
Blog and wonderful drawings of New York-based creative
director Tommy Kane.

http://www.wagonized.com/
Blog and wonderful drawings by Frances Belleville Van Stone.

http://www.theweavingloom.com/
Energetic, inspirational and very informative blog for the
modern lap loom weaver.

http://lakesidepottery.com
Informative and easy-to-follow tutorials on general ceramic
repairs and *Kintsugi* gold-mending technique from US-based
Patty Storms and Morty Bachar.

KNITTING/WEAVING

http://www.woolsack.org/BWStockists

Lists of sources & stockists of British wool yarn, fabric, fibre for spinning & felting, fleece (including raw fleece), fashion garments, accessories and textiles for the home.

SEWING AND DARNING

https://www.selvedge.org/collections/ – Selvedge (see p. 177).

BOOKBINDING

http://store.bookbinding.co.uk/store/ – Shepherd's Bookbinders. Online and retail.

ART SUPPLIES and PRINTMAKING SUPPLIES

https://www.jacksonsart.com/ – Extremely wide range of materials available online.

http://intaglioprintmaker.com/ – The destination for serious printmakers.

Rosemary Davidson
& Arzu Tahsin: http://www.craftfulness.co.uk/
               @craftfulness

Jim Boddington: http://www.jimboddingtonceramics.co.uk/
               @jim_boddington_ceramics

Ranjit Dhaliwal: http://www.studioranj.com/
               @studioranj

Jacqui Fink: https://www.littledandelion.com/
               @jacquifink

Cara Gordon: http://www.caragordon.com/
               @cara.h.gordon

Lisa Gornick: http://lisagornick.com/
               @lisagornick

Danny Gregory: https://www.dannygregory.com/
               @dannyobadiah

Chloe Healy: @chloecycles

Jo Hunter: http://64millionartists.com/
               @64millionartists

Andrea Joseph: http://andreajoseph24.blogspot.co.uk/
               @aheavysoul

Freddie Robins: http://www.freddierobins.com/
                @iamfreddierobins

Kathryn Vercillo: http://kathrynvercillo.com/artsy-side/

Acknowledgements

We'd like to thank all the makers we talked to in the course of writing *Craftfulness*, who generously shared moving and enlightening accounts of the pleasures and benefits gained from pursuing a craft practice.

With special thanks to psychiatrists Peter MacRae and Sander Kooij of the ELFT NHS North Hackney Recovery Team, Jack Holloway and Rachel Boyd at Mind UK, Paul Monks at Core Arts, Andy Cutts, Sarah Vanic and Ali Kitley-Jones at Art House, Sheffield.

In loving memory of our friend Becky Swift (10th January 1964–18th April 2017).

Permissions

Excerpts from *The Element: How Finding Your Passion Changes Everything* by Ken Robinson with Lou Aronica (Copyright © Ken Robinson, 2009). Quoted with kind permission from Viking, an imprint of Penguin Publishing Group, a division of Penguin Random House LLC. All rights reserved.

Excerpts from *Knitting Without Tears* by Elizabeth Zimmermann (Copyright © 1971 by Elizabeth Zimmermann). Reprinted with the permission of Fireside, a division of Simon & Schuster, Inc. All rights reserved.

Excerpts from *The Bookbinding Handbook* (Copyright © Sue Doggett, 2008). Quoted with kind permission from Quintet Publishing Limited. All rights reserved.